TO PRESERVE AND PROTECT

The Strategic Stewardship of Cultural Resources

LIBRARY OF CONGRESS • *Washington*

2002

Cover images, clockwise from upper left: Ages of man, from Bartolomaeus Anglicus, *De proprietatibus rerum* (Lyons, 1486); opening page of book 2, from Pliny the Elder, *Naturalis historia* (Rome, 1470); Trojan Horse from *L'Eneïde de Virgile* (Lyons, 1560); earth and its divisions, from Bartolomaeus Anglicus, *De propretatibus rerum.* Rare Book and Special Collections Division, Library of Congress.

Coin showing Janus, Roman god of beginnings, doors, and gates.

LIBRARY OF CONGRESS CATALOGING-IN-PUBLICATION DATA

To preserve and protect : the strategic stewardship of cultural resources.

p. cm.

Essays from the symposium held at the Library of Congress,

Oct. 30–31, 2000.

Includes bibliographical references and index.

ISBN 0-8444-1060-8 (alk. paper)

1. Library materials—Conservation and restoration—Congresses.

2. Archival materials—Conservation and restoration—Congresses.

3. Digital preservation—Congresses.   4. Libraries—Security measures—Congresses.   5. Cultural property—Protection—Congresses.

6. Library of Congress—Congresses.

I. Library of Congress.

Z701 .T6 2002

025.8'4—dc21

2002066140

For sale by the Superintendent of Documents, U.S. Government Printing Office
Internet: bookstore.gpo.gov   Phone: toll free (866) 512-1800;   DC area (202) 512-1800
Fax: (202) 512-2250 Mail: Stop SSOP, Washington, DC 20402-0001

ISBN 0-16-051195-X

TABLE OF CONTENTS

THE BIG PICTURE
Preservation Strategies in Context

THE SILVER LINING
Coping with Theft, Vandalism, Deterioration, and Bad Press

BUILDING THE BUDGET
*Promoting Your Program and Meeting Funding Demands
for Preservation and Security*

Contents

UNDERSTANDING SUCCESS
Measuring Effectiveness of Preservation and Security Programs

ELECTRONIC INFORMATION AND DIGITIZATION
Preservation and Security Challenges

PEOPLE, BUILDINGS, AND COLLECTIONS
Innovations in Security and Preservation

PREFACE

This volume of essays from the symposium "To Preserve and Protect: The Strategic Stewardship of Cultural Resources," held at the Library of Congress October 30–31, 2000, records an important event that complemented an array of celebratory and intellectually engaging activities held during the Library's bicentennial year. In affiliation with the Association of Research Libraries and the Federal Library and Information Center Committee, the Library turned to recognized scholars, experts, and professionals to examine some of the pressing issues facing libraries as they enter the twenty-first century. We convened outstanding thinkers from all over the world for our symposia on "Frontiers of the Mind," "Informing the Congress and Nation," "Democracy and the Rule of Law in a Changing World Order," "Poetry and the American People," and the "National Libraries of the World." These dialogues set the stage for the bicentennial symposium on preserving and protecting our cultural heritage assets.

As guardians of so much of the physical record of the past, libraries have special obligations and opportunities to preserve and protect our cultural heritage. Whereas the Library of Congress and other research libraries may have distinct—even unique—collections, we all share a common responsibility to preserve the breadth and depth of the human record. The critic Northrop Frye once said that "the only crystal ball is a rearview mirror." It has to be a wide mirror so that all forms of past expression and creativity are encompassed. Measures must be taken to ensure that this record is preserved and transmitted from generation to generation. To achieve anything less diminishes the record we pass on to our children.

To develop a strategy to address the array of concerns associated with the preservation and safekeeping of cultural heritage assets, the Library of Congress has identified four interrelated components: physical security, bibliographic controls, inventory controls, and preservation.

Traditionally, when we thought of the security of our collections, we focused on physical security controls. In developing a comprehensive collections security program beginning in the 1990s, we realized we needed to integrate the other three components as well. But physical security remains key. We must first ensure the security of our facilities so that our staff, visitors, and collections are safe. The Library has developed a comprehensive program—accelerated in the last several years because of harrowing events on our shores and at the Capitol complex itself—to enhance our physical security.

For the other three components, the Library continues expanding its programs. In 1999, we successfully launched the Integrated Library System to enhance the Library's bibliographic and item-tracking controls. In the same year, our preservation program preserved close to 500,000 items, working in a number of areas, including mass deacidification, conservation treatment, microfilming, and binding. In addition, we are developing new state-of-the-art collection-storage facilities outside of Washington, D.C., that will protect books and audiovisual materials for future generations through carefully controlled environmental conditions. These measures will serve not only our mandate to preserve the Library's collections for use by Congress and the American people, but also colleagues in cultural institutions locally, nationally, and internationally as they, too, seek to preserve and protect cultural assets.

The papers presented in this volume focus on the intersection between preservation and security. We hope that these essays might shed light on how to build bridges between preservation and security in our various institutions, and help all of us join hands in working cooperatively to preserve the record of human knowledge and creativity.

JAMES H. BILLINGTON
The Librarian of Congress

ACKNOWLEDGMENTS

The Library of Congress, joining with the Association of Research Libraries (ARL) and the Federal Library and Information Center Committee (FLICC), wishes to express its thanks to several organizations and individuals for their role in bringing to fruition the symposium "To Preserve and Protect: The Strategic Stewardship of Cultural Resources." Duane Webster of ARL provided expert advice on symposium speakers, and Kaylyn Hipps, also of ARL, coordinated with the Library on registering symposium participants. Susan Tarr, executive director of FLICC, provided staff to coordinate the project and ensure its smooth operation.

The symposium was one of several sponsored by the Library's Bicentennial Steering Committee, chaired by John Cole, director of the Center for the Book, and JoAnn Jenkins, chief of staff, Office of the Librarian. Members of the committee included Norma Baker, director, Development Office; Jill Brett, public affairs officer; Laura Campbell, associate librarian for strategic initiatives; Geraldine Otremba, director, Congressional Relations Office; Roberta Stevens, bicentennial program manager; and Winston Tabb, associate librarian for library services.

The symposium planning committee, consisting of members of the Library's Collections Security Oversight Committee, was chaired by Lynne McCay, assistant director, Information Research Division, Congressional Research Service. Members of the planning committee included Mark Dimunation, chief, Rare Book and Special Collections Division; Doris Hamburg, head, Preventive Preservation Section, Conservation Division, Preservation; Steven Herman, chief, Collections Management Division, Public Service Collections; James Schenkel, protective services officer, Office of Security; and Charles Stanhope, special assistant to the chief of staff, Office of the Librarian.

The symposium oversight committee provided guidance to the planning committee. Members included Nancy Davenport, director for acquisitions; Diane Kresh, director for Public Service Collections; Kenneth Lopez, director of security; Debra McKern, acting chief, Prints and Photographs Division; Mark Roosa, director for preservation; and Virginia Sorkin, special assistant to the chief of staff, Office of the Librarian.

The Bicentennial Program Office managed the day-to-day operations. Roberta Stevens deserves special mention for her steady and expert guidance. She was ably assisted by Robert Sokol, Web and graphic designer, and Cynthia Joy, program assistant. The office provided oversight for the three project coordinators who worked during the two years from inception to completion: Patti Fields of FLICC, who performed the initial research; Jane Caulton of the National Library Service for the Blind and Physically Handicapped, who did the research and planning; and Kathleen Eighmey of FLICC, who oversaw the final implementation of these plans.

The symposium was designed to present topics of common concern and to provide a way for participants to brainstorm on challenges and collaborative initiatives. The twenty-eight leaders of the breakout sessions underwent special training in advance of their roles to lead and facilitate those sessions. The session leaders came from the Library of

Congress, FLICC, the Smithsonian Institution, the National Archives and Records Administration, and the Department of State.

The Library's Public Affairs Office provided excellent coverage of the symposium. The Office of Special Events and Public Programs and Facility Services provided logistical support. Information Technology Services made the symposium sessions available on the Library of Congress Web site. Many other dedicated staff members throughout the Library provided assistance in a wide variety of areas, including conducting tours, making special presentations, and providing logistical support. We thank them for their responsiveness, their hard work, and their contributions in ways too numerous to recount.

And, finally, we thank those involved in the preparation of this book, a permanent record of the symposium's proceedings that can by used by those involved with cultural heritage institutions. Doris Hamburg and Andrea Merrill, Office of Security, collaborated in the initial editing, until Doris Hamburg left the Library to become director of preservation at the National Archives and Records Administration. Andrea Merrill expertly completed the editing of all papers, putting together the manuscript for the book. Linda Thomas, Office of Security, prepared the final manuscript for design and composition. In the Library's Publishing Office, Evelyn Sinclair, editor, reviewed the final manuscript, and Gloria Baskerville-Holmes managed the book's production. Susan Nedrow created the index. The book was designed by Anne Theilgard of Kachergis Book Design. Ralph Eubanks, director of publishing at the Library of Congress, oversaw all phases of publication and distribution of the book.

INTRODUCTION

At the Library of Congress, we celebrated our bicentennial throughout the year 2000 with parties, gifts, and projects that will enrich our national research collections. But no part of the bicentennial celebration was more important than our trio of symposia focusing on various aspects of our past and future contributions in working with the library community to advance the core challenges of librarianship.

In October 2000, we were fortunate to have with us national librarians from thirty-one national libraries, along with an international array of library historians, who joined in our symposium "National Libraries of the World: Interpreting the Past, Shaping the Future." That symposium was immediately followed by "To Preserve and Protect: The Strategic Steward-ship of Cultural Resource," which in turn was followed by a final bicentennial symposium devoted to the role of bibliographic control for the new millennium. It is not an accident that we chose to make this cluster of three symposia the culmination of our birthday party. For once the parties and gift-giving and celebrating were over, we knew that we must turn our full attention to maintaining this national library's vibrance and leadership in the twenty-first century. This is our true calling. And there seemed no better way to do that than by inviting our professional colleagues from various realms of librarianship to join us at the close of our birthday year to chart our collective course for the beginning of the new century.

In developing the symposium "To Preserve and Protect," we sought to engage directors, administrators, and key individuals responsible for safeguarding cultural collections in libraries, museums, and archives in a dialogue on critical issues of preserving and securing collections. Our goal was to explore concerns that lend themselves to solutions in multiple, complementary settings. Our time together provided us with a wonderful opportunity to share expertise, to discuss common issues, and to network. But most important, our chief purpose was to precipitate action, to build from our shared concerns a commitment to developing concerted programs for preserving and securing our collections.

"To Preserve and Protect" drew more than two hundred participants and included library, archive, and museum directors, preservation officers, security professionals, curators, archivists, conservators, and other decision makers from a wide variety of cultural institutions, including not just libraries, museums, and archives but also historical societies and other repositories of cultural materials. Participants came from large and small cultural institutions that are parts of universities, governments, or the private sector. Some came from professional organizations, including funding agencies. Some work independently, providing expertise and services to institutions on a project basis. Participants came from across the United States and around the globe, including Brazil, Canada, Jamaica, Malaysia, Portugal, Russia, and South Africa.

The idea and the development of the theme for this symposium came out of the Library of Congress's own recent experience. One of James H. Billington's first bold acts as Librarian of Congress was to request a thorough audit of the Library of Congress by the General Accounting Office. This audit has had many favorable outcomes for the Library, but one of the troubling recommendations from the auditors was that we should put a precise monetary value on our collections. We successfully argued that this task was both impossible—given the size of our collections and the increasing volatility of the auction market—and unnecessary, because we do not deaccession or plan to sell off our collections! But being forced to think about the collections as "assets" in this rather coarse dollars-and-cents way turned out to be useful preparation for a requirement placed on us by subsequent auditors, that we prepare an annual "stewardship report." For several years now, the Library has made a formal certification to our auditors annually about our success in safeguarding our "heritage assets," preparing just such a "stewardship report."

Determining what this lofty phrase—safeguarding our heritage assets—meant in practice turned out to be a fascinating intellectual exercise, as it led us to see, and conceptualize, some of the things that librarians do in a very different way. We determined that safeguarding our heritage assets comprised four key tasks: physical security (protecting the physical object from theft, mutilation, damage by water, fire, and so on); preservation (protecting the artifact from deterioration through conservation or reformatting); bibliographic control (knowing what collections the Library has); and inventory control (knowing where these collections are). Without any one of these legs of our four-legged stool, we could not assert that we had reasonable control over our collections.

Year by year, as thinking about protecting our assets in this holistic context has evolved, buy-in and cooperation across the institution have grown substantially. We have seen broadening ties among security, preservation, acquisitions, facilities, cataloging, and curatorial staffs as each group has needed to articulate for the others its issues, risks, concerns, and goals for safeguarding the collections. This dialogue has led us to see preservation and security as so intertwined that it would have been impossible to think of addressing one topic in this symposium without the other.

Over the last few years at the Library of Congress, we have had to face some serious issues concerning the security of the Library's collections. We experienced thefts and mutilation of the collections, subsequent inquiries from Congress, and related bad publicity. These problems were not unique to the Library of Congress, of course; but in this arena, there is little comfort in knowing you are not alone. In addressing our security problems, we had to look hard at what we were doing. We sought ways to make speedy and effective changes. We needed to invent methods for documenting success—the huge challenge of proving a negative. It was critical to convince funders that they should appropriate funds to make sure *nothing* happened—when what funders normally want to see is *something* happening—and to plot a coherent course for the future. We are confident that we are on the right track, but by no means at the end of it. In fact, we believe that there really is no end—"eternal vigilance" being not just the price of liberty, but the unending mandate for guardians of our cultural heritage.

At the Library of Congress, securing the collections has been and continues to be a process in which we learn with each step. We relied heavily on external consultants at first, while moving as rapidly as possible to create a professionally staffed Office of Security. We have worked hard to educate staff about the importance of securing our irreplaceable collections, even when it sometimes makes our work life inconvenient. We have tried to make every Library employee understand that he or she has a role to play and that this effort requires much more than just a competent police force.

I know I am not alone in regretting that security has come to play such a major role in our daily lives. We all regret that the resources that must be devoted to security continue to grow. When young librarians at the Library of Congress ask me which changes I most love and which I most regret during my twenty-eight years here, I have no hesitation in pointing—as a cause of deep regret—to the elaborate and off-putting entrance and exit security measures our visitors now face. But I also support these measures, as documented incidents of danger to staff, collections, and facilities leave no room for sentimental yearning for the "good old days."

From the early 1990s, when collections security moved front and center as a major institutional priority for us, it has been our intention to share what we have learned, and to learn from others, by focusing a brighter light in this dark corner of library and archives management. This is why protecting collections played a major role in this symposium.

Still, protecting and preserving the collections are not separate activities but an integrated process. One or even a number of actions do not solve all the collections security issues. If we are really going to be effective, we must have key preventive elements in place. We constantly need to identify and re-assess priorities, particularly in these times of shrinking or level funding. Unfortunately, it is generally easier to secure funding to cope with a disaster—whether it is to conserve a rare manuscript that is in tatters or to purchase locks and cameras for the storage room that has suffered a theft—than it is to obtain funding to maintain an ongoing program that prevents damage or loss. Although preventive programs are not generally considered to be dramatic, they are the most cost-effective, efficient, and smart. By putting into place controls and programs that prevent loss, we are doing our best to fulfill our responsibility of maintaining the collections for future generations. Prevention is thus another key theme of the symposium.

For the most part, theft and collections deterioration are both silent dangers. How can we draw attention to these problems? It is usually the spectacular theft or defacement, or the devastation that comes with flooding or fire, that captures the public's attention. It is obviously important to be as prepared as possible to react to emergencies effectively when they do happen. Most security problems, however, such as the theft of a rare book from its storage location, remain undetected for a long time. In the case of chemical and physical deterioration, such as embrittlement or damage resulting from poor handling and storage, the change is very slow indeed; and when discovered, such loss is often costly or even impossible to mitigate. Which brings us back to the importance of having ongoing programs in place to safeguard our collections through prevention and to minimize our reliance on bad news and dramatic incidents to capture the attention of our funders.

It is important that cultural institutions share understandings up front so that their funders and benefactors share expectations with them with regard to preserving and securing the cultural assets that are entrusted to them. How do funders and cultural institutions come together to move forward on a common agenda? What is the impact of publicized failures on the development of preservation and security programs?

Traditionally, when institutions suffered security or preservation problems, the approach was to try to keep the information quiet, for fear of public embarrassment. The tendency was to whisper and hope the problem would go away—or at least never again happen in our own backyards. In recent years, though, the cultural community has significantly matured in its thinking, dealing with these threats in a more forthright and collaborative manner, from which we all benefit. By making losses public, institutions have helped each other become more aware of potential risks we all share. We can take advantage of new technologies to spread such alerts more rapidly and broadly than ever before.

Throughout the planning process for the symposium, we looked for innovative approaches to the challenges facing us—challenges not only in developing programs to address preservation and security concerns, but also in selling them to our administrations and funders. How can we show that preservation and security programs are effective or necessary? Should we try to measure in a practical way how many items have not been stolen? Can we prove how we have slowed collection deterioration? How do we document success and make it as clear and compelling as the sensational stories of our occasional failures? These questions were the focus of the session "Understanding Success: Measuring Effectiveness of Preservation and Security Programs."

The subsequent session, "Electronic Information and Digitization: Preservation and Security Challenges," addressed the new and highly complex concerns that arise in regard to the preservation and security of electronic and digital collections. How will the integrity of these collections be maintained over time? Our final session, "People, Buildings, and Collections: Innovations in Security and Preservation," looked at the tension between the need to make collections accessible and the mandate to safeguard them for the future. How do we assess risks and achieve the right balance in deciding how much security or preservation is too much or too little? How do we prioritize to meet our goals?

How do we decide which artifacts to conserve and retain in their original form? How do we determine what artifacts future scholars will need in order to undertake their research, and when is saving the content in surrogate form sufficient—when is it the only realistic option? If we agree that we need to be more thoughtful about retention of certain artifacts than we have been in the past, how do we allocate responsibilities for this costly commitment in an orderly and transparent manner?

As a community, we can respond to the issues of safeguarding cultural and intellectual collections. We know from past successes with the Brittle Books Project (begun in the 1960s as a joint effort of the Library of Congress, Association of Research Libraries, and Council on Library Resources) and with the U. S. Newspaper Program (begun in 1982 by the National Endowment for the Humanities and joined two years later by the Library of Congress as a joint program) how much we can accomplish when we agree on a few national priorities and then clearly divide the labor so that each player focuses on what it does best. As we consider the future, we must share ideas on national needs, priorities, options, and the potential for cooperation among us, with a view toward developing a few action plans that could make a difference in the safeguarding of our intellectual heritage. We must both learn from each other and establish means of working with each other to "preserve and protect" our cultural resources in ways that surpass even the most effective cooperative programs of the past. Let us make that happen.

WINSTON TABB
Associate Librarian for Library Services

CULTURAL HERITAGE AT RISK

Today's Stewardship Challenge

1. Stewardship · *The Janus Factor*

Nancy M. Cline

Stewardship is a word that is appearing with some frequency in a variety of management contexts. Sometimes people ask whether it is a "softer" (or perhaps more academically respectable) term than "administration." I think not. Stewardship is the responsible use of resources; it is synonymous with managing, administering. If anything, the word implies that the responsibilities extend beyond the tenure of one single individual, that stewardship extends "over time and over generations," an appropriate expectation in the realm of cultural resources.

In using the term "Janus Factor," I want to consider the dual nature of stewardship. Most simply, the word "janus" means "having a dual function or purpose." But it is for another reason that I chose the image of Janus—the god in Roman mythology who is represented with two faces, one facing to the front and the other to the back—to describe stewardship. For Janus was "the god of gates," the guardian of doors and gates, and is often considered to preside over beginnings.

Like Janus, stewardship can be represented with two faces, one looking back upon all that has been garnered over decades and centuries and another that faces forward, anticipating, planning, preparing, and thinking strategically. Likewise, the Janus image portrays the need for security and preservation to work closely together in presiding over our contemporary "gates," so that our institutions can effectively provide stewardship of our cultural resources and ensure that they will be accessible for future generations.

I have chosen Janus because I want to think about this double-faced image in touching on some of the dichotomies we must deal with in improving our stewardship. Our roles as stewards of cultural heritage are full of both conflicting and complementary forces, ranging from the expectations of those who work in our institutions to those external constituencies whose expectations may affect public policy, legislation, institutional priorities, and governance of academic and cultural institutions.

Can most of us say that we know our role in stewarding cultural heritage? Is it at the top of the list of your administrative or managerial responsibilities? Do others acknowledge this role? Where do preservation and security fit into your strategic vision for your institution? Do you know the value of the collections and facilities within your purview? Does your staff know their value? Do you know the most valuable items or parts of your collections?

If an emergency forced you to abandon the majority of your collections, is it clear which ones should be saved? Do you have an idea what you would spend to restore or recover items? Do your budgetary commitments for the care of these collections match your rhetoric about how excellent or invaluable they are? Are there conflicts with internal institutional expectations (such as saving money on security) and the expectations of donors, scholars, or the broader public?

The Janus Factor is about leadership, about making a difference and managing risk while dealing with ambiguity. It is about maintaining focus in the midst of great cultural change. It is about being prepared for various eventualities and about expecting the unexpected. We all have strategic choices. We have the opportunity to set the expectations for an institution, to convey principles, to direct budget resources, and, perhaps most important, to raise a higher level of attention to the critical areas of preservation and security. This is not only a national priority. Given the many interrelationships among cultural and educational institutions around the globe, our strategic choices and our future actions will have an international impact.

But first, we must look at the context in which we function. Libraries exist in the continuous tension generated by the desire to provide access for users and the need to protect and preserve the collections. In most libraries, we make every effort to welcome users, though some private libraries may limit their services to a defined group of users. In libraries, guards and other security personnel generally are not evident in large numbers. Many libraries are still regarded as quiet havens for readers, safe places for research. Yet beneath a surface tranquillity, every day the collections are exposed to use from hundreds of readers and researchers, whose habits may be counterproductive to goals of preservation programs or who ignore basic concepts of security.

The challenge is to balance conflicting goals, to make materials as open and accessible as possible and at the same time to ensure that they will last for future generations. Our collections include not only books but also maps, microform materials, manuscripts, photographs, electronic resources, prints, videos, compact discs, and items in other formats. All of these formats present different vulnerabilities, different risks. Together, they hold the continuum of recorded knowledge of humankind, and, for any specific institution, they constitute a great cumulative investment, a major asset of the institution.

Despite their value, these collections may not be treated as the major investment they are. Even if the collections are closed to library patrons, staff members often work in areas located in the very midst of valuable collections. We too often assume that all our employees share a commitment to the collections and allow them to come and go through collection areas whenever needed, despite the fact that we know losses often result from internal theft. No one should be above checking. No one, not even the director, should be exempt from basic security practices.

All too often, in protecting our collections, we assume that staff members know what to look for, how to anticipate problems, how to intervene, and how to call for professional assistance when their suspicions are triggered. Although this may be a comforting assumption, staff can also be naive, anxious to assist researchers, and unlikely to identify troublesome situations or to notice unusual behaviors. Staff members may want to protect the privacy of library users, to the extent that some may be liberal in the forms of identification required in issuing privileges or likely to bend the rules for passwords so users can work directly with databases. If they do notice something odd, they may assume that security staff should not be interrupted with minor issues.

Reference skills of librarians and specialists also are likely to conflict with the need for controlling information at the scene of a crime. The propensity to find everything, inform users, and delve into details may run counter to the work of law enforcement professionals or emergency response teams. And much as we do not want to offend tourists and visitors, photography of building interiors should be strictly forbidden. Visitors photographing architectural details like doors, windows, and staircases could be documenting access, posing a threat to security.

Is it a myth that library staff members are not the best people to identify suspicious behavior? Miles Harvey in his book *The Island of Lost Maps* documents the story of map thief Gilbert Bland.

The author asserts, "He was no stranger to libraries." Not only did Bland use libraries as sources for maps, but he also used them as places to track down names of people who had died in childhood so he could create new identities for himself. Eventually, he was found out. His odd behavior and the materials he was using finally caught the attention of staff members in the Peabody Library at Johns Hopkins University. There, he had presented a fake University of Florida identification card in the name of James Perry. Throughout his many library visits across the country, he had also used the names James J. Edwards, James Morgan, Jason Pike, Jack Arnett, Richard M. Olinger, John David Rosche, Steven M. Spradling, James Bland, and Gilbert Anthony Bland (his given name was Gilbert Lee Joseph Bland, Jr.).[1] Bland had managed to blend in at many places, not arousing anyone's concern. Even when finally apprehended, he was very nearly let go, for the perception of what he had done struck the police very differently from the way it did the librarians.

"No wonder the officers did not seem particularly concerned about the meek and skittish man they found at the library. Well-dressed, polite, and obviously humiliated, he looked about as much like a menace to society as the Peabody Library looked to be a crack house. And after all, what had he allegedly done? Taken a few pages out of a book? Stolen *four sheets of paper?* There were dangerous people out there—crazy, desperate, dangerous people with guns. This poor guy hardly seemed worth the bother."[2]

When caught with the stolen maps, he offered to pay the library to repair the damaged books, and the police seemed to think this was a good deal.

Bland hit nineteen libraries, removing maps from antique atlases, from Baltimore to British Columbia. No one at these libraries had called the police, for no one had noticed their maps had been taken. And Bland nearly escaped with his offer to pay for the repairs.

When the discoveries were made known, people who had met Bland described him as "clean-cut, quiet, polite, mild-mannered."[3] He was just like so many people who come and go often in our libraries.

In library after library, neither the man nor his handiwork had been noticed. Not only that, another astonishing thing became clear. Not all the libraries from which he had stolen materials had records of ownership. The security of collections begins with accurate bibliographic records, ownership marks, and inventory practices. Security is built on many routine tasks conducted in many different parts of the library.

The work of many people can be destroyed in any one instance when library or museum objects are stolen or damaged. Building collections—selecting, acquiring, and cataloging items—can be a painstaking process, continued over decades. Often, soon after books are published, they may disappear from the marketplace, rendering them irreplaceable, or nearly so. The value of an entire collection can be greatly diminished when any one part is taken or mutilated. Destroying years of investment can take only seconds.

As we consider our roles as stewards of our cultural heritage, we must ponder not only how to secure our collections from theft and mutilation but also how to preserve them. Preservation and security are inseparable.

"Preservation is the art of managing risk to the intellectual and physical heritage of a community and all members of that community have a stake in it. Risk management is dynamic, and, in practice, preservation becomes an ever-changing assessment of value and endangerment." Abby Smith, in *The Future of the Past: Preservation in American Research Libraries* calls for collaboration between scholars and librarians as "the best and most responsible way to ensure that the legacy we have inherited, and to which we contribute, will survive into the future."[4]

"*Preservation* becomes an ever-changing assessment of value and endangerment." So what then is security but an integral part of preservation? Daily, the running of a library involves a continuum of choices and decisions (some conscious or deliberate, some instinctive or accidental), and when all are put together, our continuous involvement with both preservation and security is evident. One set of issues emerges from the moment the doors open in the morning, but the issues do not go away when the facilities are locked up at the end of the day. Then, our attention segues to different concerns. When the last janitor has shut off the lights and locked all the doors, one is still not spared all the possible accidental, environmental, or malicious threats. Pipes may leak or burst, vents can draw in fumes. The voracious appetites of bugs and rodents always present a potential hazard. Last, there is the threat posed by human beings themselves—say, the explosive or glue thrown into the book return slot.

Preservation and security frequently are set up as separate programs in different parts of the organization, each comprising many separate actions, policies, and processes. These units may easily wind up with a gulf between them, motivated by different pressures, staff working in different shifts, and competition for budget, respect, and administrative commitment. Greater benefit, however, may accrue to the institution if security and preservation work together. As an example, the Harvard College Library puts preservation, security, facilities, and information technology services under one senior administrator. A strategic partnering exists among the several units, so that they are called by one of my colleagues "the life support systems for the libraries."

As we consider the stewardship of our collections, we

must incorporate risk management in our decision making. Risk management is not just something for us to carry around in our heads. Rather, it requires conscious and continuous planning, analysis of choices, and documented procedures for action. Risk management is not an event that you do and set aside, but it is a constant process and must engage the various parts of the institution.

Recent renovations at one of Harvard's libraries turned up an envelope full of important keys in a vault that had not been used for several decades. Did someone assume that there would always be someone else to remember that the keys were there and what those keys unlocked? Suddenly finding sets of keys and not knowing what they might still open made us realize that our organization had been operating with various gaps in our security. I began to take stock of what I had assumed about people around me. I had assumed they knew it was important to care about certain things and to know whether or not some procedure was important, even though we had never specifically discussed, outlined, or defined all these things. Fortunately, we had a shared understanding about security, but we recognized a need to formalize and codify many of our commitments and priorities.

Managers should not assume that everyone accepts that preservation and security are key priorities throughout the organization. All too often, people in our organizations will readily label these concerns as someone else's problem.

Who "owns" security and preservation? Neither a preservation unit nor a security office can carry out its work as an independent contributor. Instead, each needs the support, cooperation, and behavioral and procedural change from everyone in the organization in order to be successful.

Dramatic events raise awareness of security and preservation issues. The big heists, the major cases, or the sensational thefts bring attention, but what about the other less dramatic incidents? Who cares about protecting against the small thefts, or the student observed defacing a book by highlighting or writing in it? When someone is apprehended with just a few books from our stacks that appear to have been stolen, do we look the other way? Do we shrug and say, "Well, at least they were not *rare* books?" Or, do we say, "At least we got them back?" Do we prosecute? Do we insist that fees be paid? Do we have any rules that matter? What do our reference librarians do when someone reports suspicious behavior? Do staff know what to do in such instances? Are they afraid to "bother" the police?

Likewise, do employees know how to respond when they find damaged or wet books? Do they just shrug and say, "It looks like it will hold up a bit longer?" Do they know whom to notify when they find damaged items and where to send them for repair? Are they prepared to explain to users that the condition of the book matters? Are shelvers trained to watch for mold and to respond promptly? Ignoring small problems can result in amazingly costly repairs at later stages. So it is not only "preservation" staff members who have a role in the care and well-being of the collections, but practically everyone in the library.

Small problems can grow into larger ones with security as well. Even the largest security budget can be compromised if the mailroom employees leave doors ajar to make it easier to push the cart in and out or if everyone is tolerant of Sam from the acquisitions department. We all know that he loves these collections. His loyalty is unquestioned. He works late every Friday—you have to almost throw him out of the place.

Have we factored issues such as these into our security and preservation plans? Beyond defining them as a priority, we must also ensure that all parts of the organization understand and contribute to the security and preservation of the collections. If preservation already benefits from the collaboration among preservation experts, curators, bibliographers, faculty, and others, then why should not security benefit from broad collaboration within the organization?

Libraries must deal with the inherent conflict between creating access for users and keeping their holdings secure, and they must achieve a balance between trust and watchfulness.

When faced with a theft, how do you measure the loss, and how do you set a value on the damage? How do you deal with the perception that it is "just a few pages" when the missing maps or illustrations are integral to the value of the book? When you first acquire an item for a collection, do you know whether it will become a valuable item? Perhaps the value is known to be high so it goes to a rare books area, where it is shelved with thousands of other valuable items. But the value of many items, such as collections of leaflets from Tiananmen Square, political posters from Israel, and manuscripts and correspondence from literary figures, can change dramatically over time. The prices of rare books seem to rise dramatically, making it difficult to set an economic value on a stolen item. Yet when a theft occurs, this question must be faced, even though the greatest impact is beyond the economic value.

The cultural value of these types of losses is described in an article in the 1999 *Gazette of the Grolier Club,* "The Cultural Value of Books: *United States of America v. Daniel Spiegelman, Defendant,*" by Judge Lewis A. Kaplan, relating to a theft of manuscripts from Columbia University.[5]

In her introduction to the article, Jean Ashton notes that courts frequently fail to recognize the impact of such thefts, and that these are serious crimes having consequences that could extend well beyond any monetary loss to the institution. She cites the 1998 opinion of Judge Kaplan in the Columbia case, an opinion that begins, "Great research libraries are repositories of our social, cultural, and scientific heritage. Their rare books and manuscripts are vital to understanding the world and often are irreplaceable objects of study for scholars who add to our knowledge of ourselves and our environment."

In a section on the impact of the Columbia theft, Kaplan goes on to say, "The theft of these items concededly caused economic loss to their owner, Columbia University. But the theft had an impact different in kind from a loss of money or other easily replaceable property, for these materials have value to the Columbia academic community and other scholars and, through them, to society at large that cannot be measured in economic terms alone."

I encourage you to read this article. Ashton was called upon at the hearing to elaborate on the value of an item, and she said, "The auction or appraised value is a value that is put on it by people who deal in the buying and selling of manuscripts, and that value fluctuates according to what happens to be fashionable at the time . . . scholarly value would be entirely separate."

When a loss occurs, setting the value of the missing materials is difficult. At Columbia, "appraisers were unwilling to give detailed appraisals because the materials were not there for them to examine." We are dealing now with a similar situation at the Harvard-Yenching Library. The setting of values in a theft like this becomes almost theoretical. Who knows what someone might pay for some of these rare items? Further, how do we determine the impact upon scholars and their careers?

Historically, libraries and archives have often gone to great lengths to keep silent about thefts, or to suppress information for fear of causing concern to donors. Greater openness has its benefits, however. Susan Allen in a recent article on library theft states, "Law enforcement personnel know from experience that publicity about a case will stop a thief from stealing further. The question is no longer a question of whether to notify."[6] It is now considered good practice to get the word out promptly because it may benefit other institutions, prevent additional thefts from occurring, and help one's own staff to deal with the loss. In some instances, however, advice from law enforcement professionals may argue to the contrary, where there may be reason to recommend maintaining silence or confidentiality for a period of time to build a case.

Our job is to know well before an event occurs which individuals must be involved in a response and what their respective roles are to be. It should be clear who will handle communication with the media, who is in charge of the investigation, and who needs to know which level of detail about the incident—and then to have all those people work together. By anticipating various scenarios in advance, there will be less likelihood of inept handling of the media or of the relationships with other parts of the institution, donors, or others. The actions taken in the first few hours after you realize a theft has occurred can be critical to the long-term impact on the institution. There is a stigma attached to having been a victim of theft. Often, the institution wants to avoid the negative publicity, but as many can attest, it is better to be prepared for publicity and, if possible, use it to your advantage.

How important is stewardship? To return to the cultural value of these collections, we see that the Kaplan decision states, "Spiegelman intentionally or knowingly risked inflicting, and inflicted, substantial harm not only upon his immediate victims, Columbia University and its professors and students, but also upon the greater academic community and society as a whole. In callously stealing, mutilating, and destroying rare and unique elements of *our common intellectual heritage,* Spiegelman did not simply aim to divest Columbia University of $1.3 million worth of physical property. He risked stunting, and probably stunted, the growth of human knowledge to the detriment of us all."

If a member of the judicial system and curators of rare collections can so well describe the impact of such thefts, how can we not raise our own efforts to a higher level? This calls for leadership from within each institution and for greater attention within the various professions that work in our libraries. There is much to learn from the past, yet we also have new issues to face, particularly in the digital environment, where there are growing concerns about network security and protection of digital content.

Much work needs to take place within each institution, framed according to its mission and responsive to its constituencies. We must first make security and preservation strategic priorities for our organizations so that managers and staff can carry out their responsibilities accordingly.

If the collections are among the institution's most valued assets, does the budget reflect appropriate levels of funding for preservation and security? Do you have policies for dealing with staff as well as with users whose behavior or actions are suspicious? Are you prepared to act when faced with evidence of altered bibliographic or order records? Do you have a plan for dealing with reports of theft or mutilation? When thefts occur, is the first telephone call to the police, or the university, or legal counsel, or the media? Will you allow photographs or video of the crime scene? Are staff allowed to give interviews? What do you do when a trusted book dealer calls with an item that has raised suspicion? What do you do if someone offers to recover your missing items for a "finder's fee?" What is your plan of action when an employee loses a key to the building? What are you doing to create solid working relationships with other institutional and law enforcement offices prior to needing them in an emergency?

Are your collections marked for ownership? Is there a record of those marks? Is there a catalog or other source through which you can verify ownership? Do you have records of inventories? Do you know where the rarest and most vulnerable materials are within your collections? Do you have a plan for transferring items from the stacks to locked areas when their value increases? When did you last assess the facilities? Who is aware of their strengths and vulnerabilities in the event of a disaster, including theft?

Well-trained, observant employees are key players. They are often the first ones to notice patterns or unusual behavior. If someone appears at an odd time claiming to be with "HVAC," elevator repair, or fire safety, will employees know the forms of identification to expect?

Yes, these are tedious details—but it is on the smallest of details that the success of preservation and security programs are built. It brings to mind the words of Benjamin Franklin, writing in *Poor Richard's Almanac* in 1757: "A little neglect may breed great mischief . . . for want of a nail the shoe was lost; for want of a shoe the horse was lost; for want of a horse the rider was lost."

These times call for bold leadership, new vision, and strategic thinking. The stewardship of cultural resources may be the epic challenge for the new millennium. We strive to have libraries, museums, and other cultural institutions that are both inviting and secure, that can foster access and use for education and research while preventing theft and malicious damage to some of the world's most valuable assets.

As stewards of the cultural past, we are answerable to future generations.

Our actions—as well as our inaction—form the basis for others to judge how well we are succeeding at our posts. As stewards of some of the most significant collections of accumulated knowledge and culture in the world, we must improve the ways in which our institutions manage risk.

We must provide the leadership that will make a difference, leadership that will provide focus in the midst of great cultural change. We must set high expectations and develop strong plans for our own institutions and, at the same time, work to increase the commitment to preservation and security among other cultural and educational institutions, for none of us can succeed alone.

2. **Learning to Blush** · *Librarians and the Embarrassment of Experience*

 Werner Gundersheimer

My premise is simple. It is that although the species *Homo sapiens* may have evolved well beyond the ancestor or ancestors it once shared with the anthropoid apes, modern technology has succeeded at last in making monkeys of us all.

I do not come to you as a Luddite. Far from it. Personally, I find my two computers seductive, my personal organizer and voice mail indispensable, and my cell phone addictive. My friendships, business transactions, and innermost thoughts are all communicated in ones and zeroes too much of the time. A man of the new millennium, at least a bit of it, I look upon such obsolescent twentieth-century technologies as microphotography with condescending bemusement, even while the library where I work grows increasingly dependent upon them.

Perhaps my attitudes are shared here and there in the library community. But as we all know, that community is a big tent. Whereas librarians face many common problems and embrace some similar strategies, we also have our full measure of complex and contested issues. No one—least of all someone like me, who works in a small and relatively privileged niche of our community—has a corner on wisdom when it comes to the vexing difficulties surrounding the preservation of collections. By the same token, our tent is not—nor should it allow itself to become—a closed one. Good ideas may come from many quarters, even though such ideas may find expression in terms and through venues that we might not necessarily have chosen. That is why this paper begins with, and will return to, one such source—a source that many of us might not have wished to choose.

I have a hunch that nowadays there is a name calculated to strike rage, if not terror, in the hearts of senior library administrators. That name is Nicholson Baker. Pity the poor secretary who has to tell the boss that Old Nick is on the line and has just a few questions.

That thought had occurred to me in passing after reading Baker's earlier pieces in *The New Yorker,* those dealing with the destruction of card catalogs and the diminished emphasis on books in the new San Francisco Public Library. It came to mind again in July 2000, when I finished reading his article, "Deadline: The Author's Desperate Bid to Save America's Past."[1]

For those who may have missed this lively and engaging essay—part memoir, part polemic—the deadline of its title was imposed by the British Library, which had decided to dispose of its long runs of American newspapers as of September 30, 1999, through a public sale based on sealed bids. Among these runs were complete, well-preserved bound copies of major newspapers like the *Chicago Tribune* and the *New York Sun* no longer available in any library in the United States. Some had been specially printed on archival paper.

The article describes Baker's quest for funding to buy and store these documents to keep them out of the hands of dealers who might cut them up to sell individual issues as birthday gifts. Baker also devotes much attention to a discussion of the practice adopted by many American libraries of discarding their original runs of newspapers once microfilm copies had been acquired.

It is impossible to do justice here to the vigor and intensity of Baker's essay, driven, as it is, by an intense personal commitment to the preservation of the original artifact. But it became clear to me upon reading the piece, and then even more so in the course of several conversations with the author, that he is not a man who has some weird messianic need to serve as the conscience of the library profession. That, on balance, is a good thing, because the likelihood that he could or would serve as that conscience declines in inverse proportion to his vivid and often exaggerated criticisms of it. What Baker does tell us, though—and this is a message worth taking very seriously—is that librarians and scholars are not alone in caring deeply about the issues of preservation, security, and access.

A writer like Nicholson Baker reaches a vast and influential audience, far larger and more diverse than will ever encounter the careful, thoughtful, sober analyses of our colleagues within the field. Yet many of these very colleagues, like G. Thomas Tanselle, have been saying many of the same things for years.[2]

One may or may not like Baker's style, his self-proclaimed mission, or his acerbic and not always just assessment of the work of preservation librarians, but one must admit that he is making some points—points that we ignore at our peril. I know many scholars who are grateful to be able to consult microfilm and other surrogates for original artifacts. I, however, do not know any who could tranquilly accept the notion that it is all right to get rid of all surviving copies of the originals once an adequate surrogate has been created. Everyone understands that some books and serials, once disbound or cut up for microfilming or digitization, cannot easily be reconstituted. Few agree that those particular copies have no better use than to be discarded. Most scholars would have little difficulty accepting the notion that individual copies of embrittled works need not be retained by every institution that holds one. But it would be a rare scholar indeed who would be willing to justify the wholesale elimination of all surviving copies of an embrittled work where some of those copies remained intact.

That, I take it, was Baker's main point. He found that the British Library owned long runs of important American newspapers and that those newspapers, protected in bound volumes, were, for the most part, in very good condition. The British Library had determined, through processes of its own, that it had no ongoing need for this documentation. Further, the British Library had decreed that it was really the responsibility of American libraries to maintain this aspect of the national patrimony and that it would therefore put American newspapers on the market and sell them to the highest bidder. For my part, I have no quarrel with that position, although the manner by which the British Library implemented its policy raises serious questions for the international library community.

Although the September 1999 sale certainly was not the most collegial approach in the world to disposing of an important archive—let alone preserving it—it surely reflected the British Library's conviction that no American library was likely to come forward to acquire these imprints at anything like a fair market value. Obviously, the British Library's managers knew that for decades many of our own great research libraries had been more than willing to deaccession similar runs of newspapers, thereby gaining valuable shelf space and also, at least in theory, making the materials available to readers in more compact, easily accessible forms.

In the event, the British Library's analysis was proved correct. None of our libraries did want to acquire what may well have been the last surviving nineteenth- and early twentieth-century American newspapers in something like mint condition. Even the special editions printed on durable paper apparently held little appeal for our institutional collections. The British Library assumed that the major bidders would be dealers, and, until Nicholson Baker appeared on the scene with his and his wife's retirement funds, that was indeed the case.

Now, helped by a few relatively modest foundation grants, Baker has managed to acquire at least a portion of these endangered materials. He has re-deployed his retirement fund to rent a warehouse, install shelving, and preserve the materials in New England. Some may view this as a quixotic mission, and I do not wish to appear before you as Sancho Panza to Baker's Don Quixote. However, I am pleased both that he did what he did and that he told the world about it, because in the process he has explained what makes it worth preserving, to the extent possible, the original copies of newspapers.

The decades of newspaper production between, say, 1880 and 1915 represent a period of extraordinary creativity in typography and color lithography as well as in the development of advertising and illustration in general. For all its convenience, microfilm cannot adequately preserve that aspect of the record. Baker also discovered that in the vast commercial microfilming processes, beginning in the 1930s, there were important and damaging omissions. In some cases, entire years of major newspapers were overlooked, leaving aside completely the fact that individual editions of the same newspaper embodied interesting and perhaps significant variants that are preserved on film only in very few cases.

Baker does not dispute the argument, used by many librarians in ridding their shelves of newspapers, that these artifacts are heavy and cumbersome and difficult to use. But he finds himself in much good scholarly company in pleading that despite those difficulties, a coordinated national preservation program ought to make sure that if one or two good copies of the original can be found, they should be preserved as long as possible under the best available conditions. We all know that acidic paper deteriorates at a furious rate. But we also know that under proper conditions of temperature and humidity in closed bound volumes, and subjected to only occasional use, the life of such materials can be extended for a long time.

The difficult, expensive game of preservation is, first and foremost, a game about time. As far as I can tell, there are no absolutes in preservation. The great danger in this entire area, as I believe we have or should have learned, is to place excessive faith or trust in any technology or technique that has been developed so far. That, I would suggest, was a fundamentally erroneous, if understandably optimistic assumption of many of our predecessors in this field. A similarly misplaced confidence in digital technologies could make techno-monkeys of us all.

Microfilm, coming along as it did in the 1930s, soon took its central place as the penicillin of the library world. Suddenly, diseased materials could be photographed and renewed in sterile, compact, and pristine form, while the sick old husks were discarded. Here was a permanent cure, which, while not inexpensive, could be manufactured in great quantity and made available all over the country. It also addressed a broad spectrum of maladies common to many libraries. It extended the life of their holdings and enabled human resources to be deployed more effectively and productively.

But, as with penicillin, the wonder cure was not always properly administered, some people were allergic to it, and over time it was found to be in some ways less potent than had at first been assumed. There are no panaceas in the preserving of the body and its health. Likewise, there are none for preserving the bibliographic artifact and extending its longevity.

One case in point can perhaps stand for many others. In the Folger Shakespeare Library, as in most research libraries, we have a rather sizable collection of microfilm. In institutions like the Folger, dedicated to conserving printed books and manuscripts, essentially two categories of microfilm exist: (1) master microfilms of material owned by the Folger, and (2) microfilm accessioned from other collections over the years. The first category consists of 151,350 feet of film. Of this, 76,778 feet are acetate-based film and 74,572 feet are the newer polyester film. In 1994 we suspected that there might be problems with the older acetate film, and so we obtained test strips from the Image Permanence Institute and placed them throughout the collection. Some parts of the acetate collection were clearly affected by what has come to be known as "vinegar syndrome."

At first, Folger librarians felt an unpleasant sense of panic, but later we were pleasantly surprised to discover that the collection was not as far gone as we had feared. Vinegar syndrome, however, is exponential and infectious. Some films were severely warped, and many could not be retained as regular parts of the collection.

The acetate microfilms of Folger material, however, were not true preservation copies in the sense that we had of course retained, in good condition, the original materials that we had filmed. Although it would be nice (and perhaps most cost-effective) to preserve our original acetate films, we always have the option of making a new film, and in some instances we have done just that.

Acetate films that were in reasonably good shape have now been moved to a greatly expanded cold storage facility, which represents, however, an unanticipated cost of maintaining a microfilm collection. We are next planning to splice all

Learning to Blush

acetate films of Folger materials currently stored at room temperature onto 100-foot reels. We will then make a duplicate polyester copy for public usage, discarding or replacing any films that show significant deterioration. This involves us in cost estimates, work-flow issues, and other components of a comprehensive project. Therefore, we have had to create the new position of "microfilm technician" within our Department of Photography to address some of these issues more fully.

Meanwhile, the clock is ticking. Many boxes of film in our collection emit a pungent chemical odor, signaling that slow but inevitable and irreversible process of deterioration.

Looking at the film collection as a whole—the Folger master films and the purchased films—we believe that about one-fifth of our microfilm collection may be contaminated. That means more than 100,000 feet of film. Merely identifying the scope of the problem and isolating the worst cases is a seriously labor-intensive assignment for the small staff of an independent research library.

The problem is with us like acidic paper, no better, no worse, except that our acid-paper-based holdings seem to deteriorate at a much slower rate. Now we are encouraged to believe that the newer polyester film will be our salvation, but who knows how long that will last, or what unanticipated maintenance it may in time require? Perhaps polyester will be the amoxicillin or erythromycin of the library world, losing its own potency in turn, while risking unanticipated complications.

We now stand on the cusp of an entirely new set of preservation technologies that may well bring with them an unimaginable range of unintended consequences.[3] Things, as Edward Tenner has brilliantly shown, do in fact bite back. If our great research libraries are to act responsibly with regard to preservation, they will have to assume a much more cautious stance toward the wholesale adoption of technology than they have shown in recent decades. Librarians can be justly proud of their role as perhaps the leading innovators in technology in the humanities and social sciences. For this very reason, we may also be among the first to experience the risks and perils implicit in those technologies.

The central point of Tenner's book is that we all are the victims of the unintended consequences of technological improvements. His examples range from medicine to computers and to all sorts of natural and man-made disasters, from acid rain to wood stove pollution, from the proliferation of agricultural pests to ozone depletion. It would be remarkable if libraries had been exempt from what seems to be an almost universal consequence of technological modernization. But they are not, and the issues of preservation are not limited to direct interventions such as microfilm, digitization, and deacidification.

Consider, for example, the shoddy construction practices that have come to replace far less efficient but more durable building techniques of previous generations. Nowadays, the foundation of a new library building is likely to be surrounded by an impermeable polyurethane membrane designed to keep out underground water. This replaces the much thicker and heavier construction of past eras. Strangely enough, however, the polyurethane itself deteriorates after a decade or two, thus rendering collections housed underground far more vulnerable than they would have been in another time. Similarly, fashionable architects often believe that the most elegant way to create light in a reading room is through the use of skylights. Yet the flashings and protective coatings now placed around skylights rarely last as long as the roofing materials used during periods when construction tended to be sturdier. Leaks may, and often do, ensue.

Some new technologies come with unintended consequences far beyond preservation of library materials. In the 1970s and 1980s, many libraries installed fire-protection systems using halon gas. Only later was it recognized that halon was one of the principal culprits in the destruction of the planet's ozone layer. The use of halon has since been banned, and its production has stopped, thus involving many libraries in expensive retrofitting of new fire-protection systems.

It is pointless to lament these changes, and few, if any, of us would wish to go back to an era of dusty, poorly ventilated fire traps and thumb-darkened catalog cards in creaky steel boxes. But not everything from the past is passé. First and foremost among the survivors that retain a certain currency are the original artifacts whose lives librarians have a special responsibility to prolong.

I shall never forget my first conversations with the leadership of the newly established Office of Preservation at the National Endowment for the Humanities (NEH). A relative newcomer to the library world, I was delighted to learn that the Endowment had decided to devote resources to preserving endangered materials. I proposed a grant for treating a number of fragile and irreplaceable objects in the Folger's collection, but the reply was instantaneous. "It's not our mission," I was told, "to engage in conservation of individual artifacts. We're only interested in photographing large series of embrittled materials." Although I do not know where the NEH stands on this issue at the moment, I am happy to see that the pendulum seems to be swinging just a bit toward a more balanced approach in the rest of the library community.

In Jutta Reed-Scott's excellent report, *Preserving Research Collections: A Collaboration between Librarians and Scholars,* there is a keen awareness of the need for a much more balanced approach to the treatment of books and manuscripts.[4] Reed-Scott's analysis reveals the implications of what most of us have suspected, that society is providing fewer and fewer resources to deal with a bigger and bigger problem. External funding and support of preservation have been declining steadily, while the capital costs of ramping up to new technologies continue to escalate within library budgets. Even if this were to change fairly dramatically, the agenda for most libraries would remain daunting. As Deanna Marcum wrote in the *New York Times* in 1998, "We can't save everything." But how is the triage to be effected, and who is to do it?

Too often, decisions about what is to be kept, preserved, or discarded are made at a questionable level in terms of where the expertise lies within library staffs, often without advice from other interested parties. The recent decision by the British Library to create more shelf space by eliminating 80,000 book titles seems to be a classic example, for these titles were culled by a few very junior librarians. It requires no great stretch of the imagination to suspect that useful or even important things may have gone out the doors forever in that process.

As long as we have a critical problem of resources—and there seems to be no likelihood that this crisis will end anytime soon—there remains a need for a very cautious approach to the disposition of print materials subject to deterioration. The beginning of wisdom is the recognition that all materials, not just print materials, will deteriorate eventually or could be endangered in some other way. To our collective embarrassment—we may, like many other professional cultures, have to learn to blush—print may well turn out to be the most stable of the technologies available to us. In any case, even though microfilm and digital preservation are critical to the future of the scholarly community, we need to find a way of recognizing and coming to terms with our past mistakes.

Among the benefits of modern technology is the possibility of creating an interactive database that would enable us to identify and store at least a few copies of every available printed work in the original, somewhere or other. Such a move would only begin, of course, to satisfy a critic like Thomas Tanselle, who insists that virtually every copy has something unique about it, and that nothing should be destroyed. But it would at least enable us to go to an original for additional surrogates if and when they were needed. Such a collaborative enterprise would be a fail-safe approach to what has been perhaps too headlong a leap into innovation.

To advocate this level of artifactual preservation is not necessarily to agree with Baker's assertion that the failure to do this in the case of some American newspapers has been a catastrophic mistake. But it does seem clear that our predecessors did not get it quite right. Our generation, too, and those to follow, will continue to make mistakes, for librarians are human. As such, we should be ready to blush, acknowledge error when it occurs, and move on. If we can retain a healthy skepticism about the efficacy of any given technology despite the great bandwagon effect of its commercial and institutional advocates, we stand a better chance of transmitting to those who will wish to claim it in the future the rich heritage entrusted to us.

AS STRONG AS ITS WEAKEST LINK
Developing Strategies for a Security Program

3. As Strong as Its Weakest Link

The Human Element

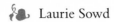 Laurie Sowd

Whether we work in a university art gallery, public library, science center, or research collection; whether we have in-house security employees, student gallery aides, campus police, or contract security; whether we rely on our collections staff and other employees to uphold security standards—the components of our security programs are basically the same: (1) staff, (2) technical systems, and (3) policies and procedures, with training tying these components together.

As the operations director at the Huntington Library, Art Collections, and Botanical Gardens, my responsibilities include security, facilities, and risk management. I have come to believe that the risk management field too often fails to take into account the crucial human element. If we have not managed people, we have not managed risk. Although each element of our security program is critical, I will focus on people, the potential "weakest link."

Specifically, I will discuss training, motivation, and development (though there are many other components of the human element, or the "people" issue, including hiring, mentoring, counseling, and others). I may select qualified people who have good work ethics, but if they are bored, they will be weak links. I can have sophisticated technical systems, but if my staff members are not trained to monitor and respond to alarms appropriately, the systems are of minimal use. I may have the most beautifully crafted policies and procedures, handsomely bound, but if my staff cannot understand them and articulate what they are, why they exist, and how to implement them, then those policies and procedures are not worth the paper on which they are written.

So, how do we manage the people in our operations? How do we keep our employees attentive, aware, loyal, and acting as outstanding stewards of the institution's assets? And, how do we measure the success of our efforts to train and motivate our staff, as indicated by how well we serve our constituents?

Let us start by looking at what motivates those responsible for the security of the collections and what creates an attractive work environment and organizational culture. The *United States @ Work 2000* study, initiated by Aon Consulting's Loyalty Institute, focuses on employee behaviors that define commitment. It identifies seven key ways by which companies can build employee loyalty: (1) enabling employees to fully develop their skills—with ongoing training to enhance their ability to feel competent and well prepared to do their jobs; (2) providing pay and benefits that truly meet employee needs (although compensation is beyond the scope of this discussion, I will address many intangible benefits we can provide our staff); (3) building a sense of spirit and pride—a sense of purpose, self-worth, and belief in the institution; (4) helping employees balance their personal needs and goals with job requirements—through social interaction, a sense of community, and belonging; (5) offering opportunities for personal growth; (6) giving to employees the same commitment we expect them to give to the organization—allowing them to take pride in the team and feel acknowledged as individual performers; and (7) demonstrating the importance of retaining employees.

To begin, we can encourage professional growth through ongoing training to enhance competence and preparedness to do a job. Management should make sure training is an ongoing process for all staff—not something that happens only during the first two weeks of employment. We should create opportunities for security officers and collections staff to share experiences. Huntington collections include art, rare books, manuscripts, ephemera, and plants, so sometimes it is difficult for security officers to recognize what objects and plants are actually collections material. Encouraging conversations between security officers and curators and conservators reaps benefits on both sides. Another factor is staff participation in volunteer and docent training. We should get officers involved in activities with volunteers. Not only does such interaction provide an opportunity to talk about issues related to collections safety and preservation, but it also raises the profile of the security function.

Some of the best career motivators come from added responsibility and opportunities for advancement. For example, ask a security officer to head a task force to look at vacation scheduling. Permit an officer to be responsible for a roll call—to select the topic, find appropriate materials, and present the topic or arrange for a guest speaker to do so. We can also identify and post a different training topic for each month, tying our selection of guest speakers and activities into the theme. For example, during "collections" month, discuss theft response, have a preparator talk about object mounts and review collections movement policies, have your facilities staff discuss temperature and humidity monitoring, and invite the public relations staff to discuss the scope of the collections from the point of view of institutional image.

We should consider a "formal" certification for completion of a set of programs. Programs could include videos to watch, one-on-one training with a supervisor, presentations by collections staff, and so on. Programs can be self-directed and should be based on an assessment of what competencies are important to the protection of the institution's assets. Recognize completion of the certification path by presenting the officer with a lapel pin to be worn on the uniform.

Do your officers understand how to move up in the organization? Do they know what skills are needed and how to acquire and demonstrate them? You might initiate a "mystery shopper" program with a sister institution. Have a new security officer observe officers at the other institution anonymously from the visitor's or scholar's perspective. Provide guidelines on what to look for in behavior and deportment, what to ask, and what to do. Debrief your officer on the way security officers behaved at the other institution. Discuss the skills that enhance performance.

In building spirit and pride and belief in the institution, we can encourage our staff to feel part of the mission in several ways. Staff members should understand the institution's mission and be able to articulate it. Do you have related mission statements for security and preservation? If not, how about developing such mission statements with your staff, to create focus and buy-in to the mission? The Huntington and Getty museums' security mission statements are such examples. At the Huntington,

> Adhering to the highest ethical standards, the security department provides for the security and safety of the visitors and staff and protects and preserves the collections and other assets of The Huntington. We facilitate an enjoyable experience for all visitors and a pleasant work environment for staff. Acknowledging the theme of education in The Huntington's institutional mission statement, the security department recognizes its duty to inform and educate staff and visitors about security and safety issues in order to sustain and promote the continuing welfare

of the institution and its collections. The department provides these services with diligence, efficiency, thrift and politeness. The administration of The Huntington supports and encourages the security department in its pursuit of the goals put forth in this mission statement.

The Getty's mission statement promises a commitment "To safeguard and protect the visitors, staff, collections, and facilities of the Getty through a combination of security and emergency procedures, technology, and trained personnel."

We must provide information about the institution to security officers to help create buy-in to the organization. Invite guest speakers to your roll calls or department meetings. Consider inviting those inside your institution, such as curators for exhibition previews, educators for new family programs, the president of the institution, and the public relations manager—as well as those outside the institution, such as the local fire chief or the construction foreman working on a project at your institution. Relay monthly attendance statistics, visitor and staff accident information, and updates on construction projects. Beware the attitude of the telecommunication's organization supervisor who said, "We know that communication is a problem, but the company is not going to discuss it with the employees."

The Ritz Carlton, in another example, emphasizes the positive power of words in dealing with clients. It is important to view both visitors and staff as key clients. What impression do you get when you hear that "Our policy is . . ." versus what you feel when told, "I apologize for the inconvenience?" How about, "I am not allowed to . . . ," versus "How can I help?" Keep in mind what words say about the department's philosophy toward dealing with its many clients.

Balancing personal needs with job requirements—to build social interaction and a sense of community and belonging—starts with the fact that "All work is social—a fact of work life that people ignore at their peril." So says Lois P. Frankel, a business coach and senior partner at Corporate Coaching International in Los Angeles, California. "Establishing good working relationships can help us secure the cooperation of the people we need to accomplish our tasks. If we delay building good relationships until we really need them, it will be too late." Some of her favorite techniques include dropping into someone's office once a day for a ten-minute talk or greeting security officers by the timeclock for a chat about their families or vacation plans. Casual conversation helps build friendly relationships that can withstand stress. When people talk to you, listen—put everything else on hold. Begin conversations with small talk—so people know you care about them, not just their work.

We should acknowledge that our staff members have private lives. Consider rewards that appeal to a staff member's leisure time activities—movie tickets or restaurant gift certificates. Sometimes sending a card to the staff member's significant other is appropriate. Do not be the shipping executive who asked an employee to reschedule her sister's funeral to a day that "would be better for me."

Whenever possible, schedule all-staff activities at a time when officers can attend—right before their reporting time, for example. Otherwise, consider rotating attendance—free up two officers this time, two different officers next time.

To create opportunities for personal growth—another important element in staff engagement—we should strive to make the work more interesting. A career as a security officer may very well seem inherently boring. To fight that, try rotating posts through and within buildings. Rotations can occur within a single day, day to day, week to week, or even less frequently, but give people something different to look at and a way to fight the tendency to become immune to their surroundings. As an added benefit, new eyes looking at the same area may result in suggestions for improvements.

If you have regular meetings or roll calls, hold some of them "in the field," at construction sites, exhibit installations, or tricky access points. During training sessions or roll calls, get out the grab bag. Have your security officers write down questions they are most frequently asked. Take other questions from complaints or suggestions on comment cards, the communications or public relations department, receptionists, and visitor surveys. Write a single question on each slip of paper, creating as many slips as you want and putting them into the grab bag. During training sessions, have a security officer draw, read, and respond to the question, and then follow with a helpful critique from you and from officers present. Instead of slips of paper, the Getty uses laminated flash cards, color-coded by topic, that can be used by supervisors with officers, or as self-study aids. The flash cards can be used for training exercises that test the officer's knowledge of steps to take in a specified situation.

Role-playing, too, can be a useful training device. Develop and stage brief scenarios (thirty seconds to two minutes) relevant to your environment. Use your enthusiastic problem-solvers (your security officers, volunteers, or others) to create scenarios and to perform in them. For example, pretend a visitor tries to take a flash photograph in the manuscripts gallery. Create a situation in which everyone wins—where the security officer stops the visitor from taking flash photographs, but the visitor retains his or her dignity and good feelings about the organization. Focus on the "win-win" scenario, but show "losing" scenarios, too. Consider videotaping sessions for future use.

To keep hourly employees engaged and alert, it may help to rotate staff members to other departments for a half-day. Have a security officer spend some time in the stacks, and rotate a collections staff member from the stacks to a bag checkpoint.

A scavenger hunt can be a fun, effective, and quick way to ensure that security officers remain knowledgeable. One natural area to focus on is the location of visitor-service-related subjects, particularly for new staff orientation: where visitors can fill out comment cards; where the X exhibition is; where restrooms and drinking fountains are located; where Y special painting is located; where to go for information on Z; and so on. Have security officers retrieve a marker from each location to prove they found the right destination. Or, scavenger hunts can focus on the location of fire extinguishers, emergency exits, or water leak response kits.

We need to find ways to give to employees the same commitment we expect them to give to the organization—an ability to take pride in the team and also feel acknowledged as individual performers. In the Denver Museum of Natural History's customer service department, staff members found that their services were well rated by visitors, providing them an opportunity to take pride in the team. As a result, the staff decided to aim higher, to put a fine polish on those services by improving staff morale and job satisfaction, focusing on the individual performer. The underlying assumption that happier people are more effective and make better representatives for our institutions works from a security perspective. Staff members who enjoy their work and take pride in it make more invested and alert guardians of the collections. The museum's efforts included involving staff members in crafting their own job descriptions and evaluation criteria and in providing more frequent, informal evaluations of those staff members.

It is important to find opportunities for public recognition through staff newsletters, roll calls, and department meetings. The "Practical Supervision" newsletter from Professional Training Associates recommends starting each week with a list of your employees. As soon as you notice an employee doing something that merits recognition, make a note beside the person's name. Add a big check mark as soon as you congratulate the person for his or her accomplishment, something that should be done right away. Pay special attention to people who still do not have a check mark by Thursday, and find a contribution to recognize.

The Science Place in Dallas, Texas, launched a "Wow!" program. When a staff member goes above and beyond the call of duty, the person who recognizes the achievement gives the staff member a coupon redeemable for small prizes and an employee-of-the-month recognition (provided through the organization). Both the recipient and the giver are appreciated for values honored by the organization: innovative ideas, creative problem solving, honoring of cultural diversity, superb communication, and so on. Likewise, the "Shining Star" program at the Shedd Aquarium provides a pin and recognition breakfast for high achievers.

If your security officers already wear name badges, add an indication if they are bilingual (e.g., "Officer Jones, Yo hablo Espanol"). The officer is proud of his or her extra capabilities, the staff recognizes that special skill, and visitors receive appropriate assistance. Other ways to emphasize staff teamwork include taking an annual department photograph to post or to distribute to other staff online; providing opportunities for a public round of applause, such as at staff holiday lunches, all-staff meetings, and department meetings; and asking people what rewards are meaningful to them. Go straight to the source to find out what motivates your staff members.

It is also important to show commitment to retaining employees by communicating that the institution values high-achieving employees. Assess staff turnover to see how successfully you are retaining those staff members. Does the rate of preventable terminations exceed that of other departments or the institution as a whole? Does it exceed last year's figures? Does it exceed an industry benchmark?

We have looked at ways to keep our staff motivated and attentive. Now, how do we know whether our efforts are paying off? How do we measure success in meeting our organization's objectives through an invigorated staff? At the Huntington, the security manager and I jointly determined who the security department serves and what those constituents want. We then crafted some basic security objectives—the fundamental responsibilities of the security function—and agreed on ways to measure progress against these objectives. We developed five broad objectives for our security organization and established ways to measure our success:

(1) The Huntington experiences no collections, buildings, or property damage or loss that reasonably could have been anticipated or mitigated by security actions. This is measured by loss experience.

(2) Huntington staff members—and also readers, volunteers, and others—perceive that the security department adds value to their work life and work environment. Added value is measured by discussions with staff members or surveys of staff attitudes, reports to the safety log, and incident reports. Elements here include the following:

- Staff members feel safe and secure at work.
- Staff members receive appropriate and reasonable assistance from security officers, consistently and promptly.
- Staff members perceive that security-related policies and procedures are reasonable and fair.
- Staff members perceive that the security of the institution is rigorous and appropriate for the people and property protected.

(3) Huntington visitors perceive that the security department adds value to their visit. Visitor reactions are measured by discussions or surveys with visitors, and by comment cards. We want to determine that:

- visitors feel safe and secure on the property;
- visitors feel welcome; and
- visitors receive accurate and helpful information from security officers.

(4) Senior management of the Huntington perceives that the security department is efficiently, effectively, and credibly led by security management staff. Leadership is measured by turnover and retention ratios, through observation of the general ledgers on a quarterly basis, and through discussions with principal security officers. Our goals are to ensure that:

- High-achieving security officers are retained.
- The combined operating and salary budget in the security department is consistently within 1 percent of the budgeted bottom line.
- Senior management perceives that it is valuable to involve security officers in discussions, problem-solving, and response to emergency situations.
- Senior management can see that the security department handles both day-to-day operations and special programs—such as exhibits, events, and lectures—with a high degree of professionalism.

(5) Security officers perceive that the Huntington adds value to their lives and that they in turn add value to the organization. Such staff perceptions can be measured by discussions or surveys with security officers. We expect our discussions to reveal the following:

- Security officers feel they are well trained. They clearly understand and can articulate their job responsibilities.
- Security officers feel they have opportunities for growth.
- Security officers feel they contribute to the organization and are respected and appreciated for that contribution.

In our discussion, we have not yet used one key word—judgment. We build employee commitment through training and organizational philosophy so staff members understand what is expected of them and why. Then, we must let our employees exercise judgment within those parameters. This is crucial—"the institution has trained you well and trusts you to act in its best interest." The effort to strengthen the human element of our security programs can never ebb. It must be our constant mantra, for people can easily be our greatest asset, rather than our weakest link.

4. Developing a Plan for Collections Security · *The Library of Congress Experience*

 Steven J. Herman

The Library of Congress has developed a comprehensive, integrated collections security program to protect its "heritage assets" (the term we have given to the Library's permanent collections). Keys to success in building this program consisted of: first, recognizing the challenges facing us; next, obtaining management and staff support; and, finally, ensuring a collaborative effort between security and library professionals. Neither library managers nor security professionals, operating alone, could have produced the high-quality program that we developed in this collaborative environment. The result is a program that not only has widespread buy-in but also has a readily understandable implementation phase—because staff members are on board and understand the concepts, terminology, and need.

As we began developing a collections security plan for the Library of Congress, we realized that the program would be successful only if we first made a realistic assessment of the existing situation. In so doing, we found challenges that we needed to recognize and address. I believe there were four main issues:

(1) "It's not my job." Although not always apparent, the Library's culture betrayed an attitude of "we versus they" between the Library's staff and managers and the Library's security professionals. Although not antagonistic, this attitude often took the form of staff members' feeling that they should not be asked to assume the responsibility for collections security but, rather, that this was the job of the security professionals. Staff members felt that they themselves had been hired and trained to help researchers and build collections, not to enforce security regulations and act as police.

(2) "All this money and not one book." At the same time that everyone agreed that security was necessary, Library staff members often resented the amount of money spent on security, believing that it took away funds from such core Library activities as reference and collections development. It was not unusual to hear a staff member say that we are spending a lot of money on security, but all that money does not buy us one manuscript or one book.

(3) "Security is locks and cages." Traditionally, when we had talked about collections security, people immediately focused on physical security—that is, lock-and-key control, surveillance cameras, intrusion detection, cages, and vaults. We believed that effective collections security, however, required a much broader-based program than simply physical security, and that if we defined the program more broadly, we also would attain increased interest and buy-in from Library staff.

(4) "Don't you trust us?" We believed that an effective security program should address all possible threats. For collections security, this involved changing procedures for access to the collections both for researchers and for Library staff. Perhaps no other aspect of developing our program evoked the level of emotional reaction, especially from staff, as we saw when we modified our policies to limit staff access to collec-

tions storage areas in 1992, shortly after closing the stacks to the general public.

We addressed these four main challenges and made every effort to enlist the support of the staff:

(1) "It's not my job." Those of us who have witnessed the mutilation and theft of irreplaceable items—and have seen the frustration of researchers who have traveled long distances for an item that can be found only at the Library of Congress, arriving to find the item either missing or mutilated—are convinced that security is everyone's job. We have adopted a concept of levels of responsibility, with the staff being the first line of defense. When the situation cannot be addressed safely and satisfactorily by the staff member, or when the event happens outside of a reading room or work area, we summon the Library of Congress Police.

We have established an active security awareness program to make staff members aware of the importance of collections security and of their role in ensuring the protection of our heritage assets for this and future generations. Examples of successful initiatives include: regular articles in the staff newsletter, the *Gazette;* programs for the staff such as a Security Awareness Week, with posters, bookmarks, and presentations; presentations to groups of employees; and displays of mutilated items, including the cost of the items and the unique information or illustrations that were lost.

(2) "All this money and not one book." This concern is voiced more frequently in an era of diminishing resources and increased competition for available funding. We have explained to our staff that the result of not spending the necessary funds to protect our heritage assets can be far worse in terms of mutilation, theft, and permanent, irreplaceable loss of the artifact and the information than the reduced purchasing ability that may result from allocating funds for security pur-

poses. Staff awareness has been increased by displays of mutilated items and, wherever possible, by sharing stories of attempted thefts and mutilations that were thwarted by having alert security staff. In collections areas having a high value and unique material, success stories can significantly raise staff awareness and understanding of the need to have adequate security staff.

(3) "Security is locks and cages." Perhaps one of our major accomplishments as we crafted our comprehensive collections security plan was to move away from the traditional view that a collections security program equates with a physical security program—locks, keys, cages, security cameras, intrusion detection systems, alarms, and so forth. Indeed, as we developed our collections security program, we took a much broader approach. We felt that a truly comprehensive plan must address four critical issues: what we have, where each item is at any given time, how we preserve the items for this and future generations, and how we protect the items physically. Only the last of these four issues—physical security—has traditionally been addressed by the security professionals; the other three are traditionally addressed as core library activities—bibliographic control, inventory control and tracking, and preservation. By defining collections security as including all four areas, we were not only able to put together an integrated plan but also to bring professional librarians and security experts together in this collaborative effort.

(4) "Don't you trust us?" We took a number of positive steps to explain to the staff why it was necessary to make certain changes; even so, we were not completely successful in convincing everyone on the staff that we had to adopt the policies we did. Among the steps we took were the following:

- We held a number of staff forums in which the Librarian of Congress and security and other Library staff members explained to Library employees what we were doing and why.

- As part of these forums, we set up dramatic displays of mutilated items with captions that explained the uniqueness of the items, what had been lost and could never be examined again, and the assessed cost of the items. Staff members attending these forums and viewing these exhibits left with a very different perspective of the scope of the problem and the impact of not protecting the collections than they had had when they arrived. By showing concrete examples, we demonstrated that mutilation and theft were not mere abstract concepts.

- We established options to determine stack access for staff in various positions to ensure that staff members could continue to do their work without encountering significant roadblocks in their path, and we explained these options to the staff. We tried to remain as flexible as possible in listening to the concerns of staff and in developing appropriate options.

- We were honest with staff members in reaffirming our belief to them that they are our greatest asset and that we were not accusing them of dishonest behavior. At the same time, all of us needed to recognize that out of a staff of more than four thousand employees, it only took a few people to create serious damage to the collections. Unfortunately, there was no "profile" that we could use to determine who might create problems and therefore restrict access only to those individuals. We shared with staff specific incidents involving staff, as well as citing studies and articles supporting the need to address insider as well as outsider threats.

Once we had both librarians and security professionals working collaboratively, our next step was to develop a framework that we hoped would cover all four control areas: bibliographic control, inventory control and tracking, preservation, and physical security. We did so by adopting a series of four steps that, when completed, would constitute the collections security plan itself.

Step 1: Reaffirming the four categories of controls. This was a fairly straightforward process. We agreed—and our consultants and auditors supported our understanding—that our collections security plan would provide a program to assert:

(1) *Bibliographic control.* This is the most logical first step: we need to know what we have—primarily author and title information.

(2) *Inventory control and tracking.* Once we know what we have, we need two additional pieces of information: how many we have and where each item is assigned (for instance, the Law Library, general collections, or Main Reading Room reference collection); and the location of each item if it is moved from its assigned location (for instance, for circulation or rebinding).

(3) *Preservation.* Once we are satisfied that we know what we have, and where each trackable item is at any given time, as stewards of the nation's "library of last resort," we need to ensure, through best preservation techniques, that the item will be available not only for the current generation, but also for future generations. Preservation measures include components such as: regulating and monitoring the environment; emergency preparedness; proper furniture and equipment; proper handling; physical treatment; and reformatting.

(4) *Physical security.* Finally, we could not underestimate the importance of ensuring that the item is physically secure, especially when in its storage location. We therefore looked at vaults, cages, cameras, limited-access stacks,

intrusion detection, and other means to secure the collections.

Step 2: The tiers of risk. One of the most challenging aspects of putting together the collections security plan was to establish the tiers of risk. By categorizing material into one of five categories along the tiers-of-risk continuum, we were acknowledging that all collections items are not created equal for the purpose of developing a meaningful security plan. With finite resources, and 120 million items in our collections, it is essential that we categorize material so that we can determine how best to deploy our resources to ensure the protection of collections according to their value (not simply monetary value, but also research, uniqueness, and artifactual value). We could not examine, make a meaningful determination, and provide a protection program for every one of the 120 million items in the Library's collections, but we could establish broad categories to form the tiers of risk. From our discussions, we developed a five-tier risk continuum, and we labeled the collections accordingly:

(1) *Platinum.* These collections essentially include the Library's most priceless items. The "Treasures" are the quintessential components of this category.

(2) *Gold.* These collections include the Library's rare items having prohibitive replacement cost, high market value, and significant, cultural, historical, and/or artifactual importance.

(3) *Silver.* These collections require special handling and include the Library's items at particularly high risk, such as computer software, popular labels in print, videos, and compact discs.

(4) *Bronze.* These collections include those items served without special restrictions in the Library's reading rooms and materials that may be lent without stringent restrictions.

(5) *Copper.* These collections are those that the Library does not intend to retain but holds while deciding, for example, which items may be used for its exchange and gift program.

Step 3: Establishing the life cycles: Our next discussion involved what the status of an item might be at any given time. We identified five possibilities:

(1) *In Process.* Refers to the collections while held during their accessioning, organizing, processing, and transport to storage.

(2) *In Storage.* Refers to the collections while in permanent storage.

(3) *In Use.* Refers to the collections while being used by researchers or staff.

(4) *In Transit.* Refers to the collections while being transported from permanent storage to another location.

(5) *On Exhibit.* Refers to the collections while on exhibit either at the Library of Congress or at another location.

Step 4: The security control measures—developing the grids. Our next step was to identify, for each tier of risk and each life cycle, the security control measures that would be used to protect the collections. The security control measures were aimed at responding to the four questions discussed earlier: what do we have (bibliographic), how many of them and where are they (inventory control and tracking), how do we preserve the items (preservation), and how do we physically secure them (physical security)?

We began with the physical security requirements, because physical security has received the greatest attention and is the most straightforward to address. To ensure a collaborative effort and buy-in, we put together a team of physical and electronic security specialists and library managers who had already played a major role in collections security planning. The team identified and defined the measures that should be taken to protect the collections. In the area of physical security, these measures included: marking (ownership) and tagging (theft detection strips); secured transit; intrusion detection; closed-circuit television; storage; key and lock control; electronic access control; and exit inspection. For many of these measures, we established levels of control depending on the tiers of risk. For example, for closed-circuit television coverage, we had three levels. Level 3, the highest level, was defined as "image displayed and recorded in Library police communications center during alarm condition." Level 2, the intermediate level, was defined as "Level 1 with additional cameras capturing facial features plus specific areas of interest, for instance, patron using material at desk in Rare Book and Special Collections Reading Room." Level 1, the minimum level, was defined as "recorded cameras showing large area views with limited facial details of individuals."

When we had completed this process, we had five grids, one for each of the life cycles—in process, in storage, in use, in transit, and on exhibit.[1] One of the most challenging steps followed: determining which level of control applied to which tier in each life cycle. Our guiding principle was to answer the question, "What is the minimum requirement that we need to implement to be able to satisfy ourselves that we can give assurance that the collections are being protected to the appropriate level?" In this context, we once again had to develop and accept a number of working assumptions:

- There is no such thing as absolute assurance. Although we can have a policy of zero tolerance for those stealing or mutilating the collections, we cannot give absolute assurance that nothing will ever be stolen or damaged.

- Not every item can be protected to the same level, nor should it be, given finite resources. Our program must aim at giving assurance that the appropriate level of protection is being provided. Certainly, the nature and level of protection for the Library's copy of the Gutenberg Bible is not the same as that given to today's edition of the *New York Times*.

- We therefore needed to establish the minimum level of security for each specific category of material. We were cognizant of the fact that our collections security plan, when finally developed, would be presented to our peers, management, and others. Credibility was key if the plan was to be accepted and was to serve as the basis for an implementation program. We needed to ensure that our security program could indeed be supported and could serve as the basis for future planning, programming, and budgeting.

Once we had completed our protection prioritization framework of physical security controls, we were ready to gain broad-based acceptance. First, we gathered a group of our peers together and presented the proposed plan. We explained it, received their feedback, and made modifications as appropriate. Next, we presented the plan to the Library's senior managers and got their feedback and approval. And, finally, we received the approval of our congressional oversight committees. The last was accomplished in early 1998.

Our planning groups were intent on ensuring that the plan, as finally adopted, would serve as a guide for action and would not be just another study to sit on the shelf. For that reason, we developed a set of actions, a timeline, and four standing subcommittees to lead the implementation phase. The four areas represented by these subcommittees are: Policy and Standards; Operations; Security Awareness; and Resources. These subcommittees meet regularly, and the chairs of each gather periodically to share progress and ideas.

Establishing minimum standards was important. But the

next step we needed to take was to assess where we are, and what we need to do to meet these standards. Our assessment program consisted of visiting all the custodial and processing divisions and discussing the program with them. These field visits and the personal interaction proved to be a wise way to proceed and yielded excellent results. In discussing what we needed to obtain during these visits, we went back to our grids and looked at the dots we had placed in the matrix indicating the minimum standard. We decided that wherever a dot was present, we would replace this during our field visit with a baseline status, i.e., stating how well that specific custodial or processing unit met the minimum requirement. To aid us in gathering data, we identified five baseline statuses:

C, or completed, meaning that the division meets the minimum standard.

P, or partially completed, meaning that additional actions will be required to meet fully the minimum standard.

F, or funded, meaning that although controls are incomplete at this time, monies to create controls meeting the minimum standard have been appropriated.

H, or "in-house," meaning that the division currently does not meet the minimum standard but can do so by reconfiguring with no additional funding.

U, or unmet, meaning that the division does not completely meet the minimum standard.

We then conducted our visits, filled out the grids using the statuses above, and elaborated on these with comments. The grids prepared for each of the Library's custodial and processing divisions continue to provide the framework for security planning as we implement the minimum standards we established in the plan.

The approach we adopted was highly successful on many levels. I believe the greatest advantages are:

- *Collaborative effort.* The development and implementation of the collections security plan was a collaborative effort of Library managers and security managers and staff. I cannot emphasize enough the importance of this collaboration. It built mutual trust and understanding, when there is traditionally a kind of wariness. By presenting this plan as a collaborative effort, Library staff and managers more readily accepted it.

- *A shared vocabulary.* By getting away from an extended list of formats, value, and specific collections assignments, and by using five categories of tiers of risk that are not dependent on format or custodial unit, managers and staff throughout the Library have adopted the same vocabulary. If we say that we have developed a project to protect the *gold* collections, staff members understand what we are doing.

- *An approved, understandable plan.* A major challenge that we have faced in the past has been that, although we have long taken collections security very seriously and have a zero-tolerance policy for theft and mutilation, we did not have a formal plan to which we could refer when preparing budget requests or when deciding which collections security initiatives we should tackle first. Without such a document, we had not always been articulate or convincing in implementing collections security measures. Now we can refer to the plan when developing a program to enhance collections security.

- *A blueprint for action.* We found, as we went from division to division, that many of the minimum requirements had already been met, that others were in the process of being met, and that others could be done in-house. For those unmet needs that require additional funding, it is far more meaningful to place these in a multiyear plan along with prioritization (protecting our platinum and gold collections first, for example). Our requests are far better received when they fit into a planning framework than when they come as disjointed requests.

- *A synergistic approach.* We found that—in determining what to implement, how to implement it, and what might be unattainable—we needed to look at the plan in its entirety, rather than blindly following each minimum requirement. In so doing, we established two basic principles. First, a synergistic approach is essential because if we cannot meet a minimum requirement in one area, we may be able to use controls in place in another area to provide the same level of assurance that we are protecting our collections. Second, as good as a plan is, there is no substitute for good judgment.

5. Creating a Culture of Security in the University of Maryland Libraries

Charles B. Lowry

In mid-October 2000, the University of Maryland libraries had an object lesson that illustrates that building a culture of security is still a work in progress. Despite improvements in procedures and security awareness instituted in recent years, we still have a long way to go. In the October incident, a young man had walked out of the front entrance of the University of Maryland's McKeldin Library carrying a computer monitor. No one questioned him. The incident, however, occasioned a considerable amount of discussion on the staff e-mail.

A few days later, the same young man was stopped carrying the associated computer processor unit and questioned by a staff member. It is a relief to report that he was a graduate student cleaning out his carrel and the equipment was his own. Nonetheless, this anecdote illustrates both (1) the challenges we face in developing an effective safety and security program in a large research library, and (2) the progress we are making in improving security awareness among staff.

Although significant safety and security problems are relatively infrequent in academic libraries, all library staff members need to maintain a keen awareness of the fact that they are working in a busy environment that is open to the public many hours a week. Moreover, those of us in academic and public libraries are part of a larger community, where thousands of people live, work, and go to school every day. To be responsible members of this community and to protect our patrons, staff, collections, and facilities, we must all share responsibility for safety and security. Libraries are "systems," and security is a vital part of maintaining balance in these systems.

Safety and security in libraries include a diverse range of topics, from the seemingly mundane—such as enforcing a no-food and no-drink policy—to more serious incidents that include theft and disruptive behavior. Therefore, it is important to provide staff with the information and the tools they need to respond to a variety of situations. Staff members need clearly stated policies and procedures and the training to understand them so they can take action when called upon to do so—in what might be called a shared culture of mutual responsibility for security and safety.

In 1997, the University of Maryland libraries embarked upon an assessment of its policies, procedures, and facilities in partnership with the Association of Research Libraries (ARL). The security study and subsequent development of practice and policy were implemented over a two-year period and model a comprehensive approach for a large academic library system.

The safety and security environment in the fall of 1997 was long overdue for some scrutiny. For several years, the libraries had contracted with the University of Maryland Police Department (UMPD) to recruit, train, and manage Student Police Aides (SPAs). Frequently undergraduates, the SPAs were posted at the entrance of the two largest library buildings, McKeldin and Hornbake, and they also staffed a security point in the "twenty-four-hour room" on the ground floor of Hornbake. At both libraries, their principal duties were to monitor the electronic theft-detection gates at the exits, enforce the no-food and no-drink policy, and be on the lookout for disruptive behavior. At the four smaller branch libraries on campus, SPAs were employed only at closing time, when they would perform sweeps to ensure that all patrons had vacated the facilities.

In September 1997, the UMPD indicated that it wished to terminate the SPA contract with the University of Maryland Libraries because it found it difficult to recruit, select, train, and retain an adequate number of SPAs to meet the contract. Further, the UMPD was frustrated with the criticism that resulted from the many shortcomings in the service. For instance, SPAs often did not show up for duty on time; they did not enforce the no-food and no-drink policy; and they slept on the job. In retrospect, it is clear from the dearth of incident reports that the SPA system did not really provide security, but only the illusion of security. Unfortunately, this arrangement was more of a security blanket that allowed us to avoid taking full responsibility for library safety and loss prevention.

The UMPD's position and the arrival of new leadership in the library provided the occasion to review this practice. As the newly appointed dean of libraries, I worked with the new director of public services to reevaluate the situation. Philosophically, we agreed that the staff should assume the principal responsibility for safety and security of library users, collections, and facilities. Indeed, we noted more than once the irony of having undergraduates deal with sensitive and often difficult matters while full-time staff members remained outside observers. Candidly, although staff members were not anxious to take on the job themselves, they were willing to complain loudly when an SPA failed to open up a facility or fulfill any small duty.

Pragmatically, we were interested in reallocating the funds that went into the SPA contract for other staff needs. As chance would have it, the Association of Research Libraries, located in Washington, D.C., was seeking to pilot a security self-study with a nearby member of the association, and the University of Maryland was approached. Because the ARL proposal would give us an opportunity to make a top-to-bottom review of our safety and security capabilities and to explore alternatives, we were eager to participate.

After some negotiation, the ARL project commenced in October 1997 with a meeting between the Library Executive Council (senior managers reporting to the dean), Glenn Zimmerman from ARL, and Robert Morse from George P. Morse and Associates, a local loss-prevention firm hired to consult on the project. Morse and Associates would conduct a comprehensive audit of the University of Maryland libraries' safety and security environment as a foundation for developing self-study materials that might also be used in other libraries. The audit would be both a management study—focusing on philosophy, policies, and procedures—and an assessment of existing facilities and practices, with recommendations for corrective action as needed. Morse presented the libraries a project proposal in November with an anticipated completion date of April 1998. The director of public services and the director of planning and administrative services were designated as the in-house contacts for the audit. Throughout the project, we remained in regular communication with the Association of Research Libraries.

Shortly after we began the audit in 1997, the UMPD informed us that if we wished to continue our contract, there would be a dramatic increase in charges for SPA services once the contract expired at the end of the year. Rates were to increase nearly 200 percent from eight dollars per hour to fifteen dollars per hour, a figure that the libraries' budget could not sustain. In anticipation of that eventuality, and in recognition that the audit and its recommendations would not be available until spring, Hornbake Library security was turned over to the Hornbake circulation staff. We continued to use the services of the SPAs at a negotiated rate of twelve dollars per hour in McKeldin Library, with the proviso that we would terminate the contract if the recommendations of the audit pointed us in a new direction.

Morse and Associates conducted numerous site visits and interviews in late 1997 and early 1998, including meetings with the UMPD, facilities personnel, campus security, security-related vendors such as 3M (Minnesota Mining and Manufacturing), and numerous library staff. These meetings were intensive in-depth considerations of the environment. In addition, Morse conducted a thorough investigation of six library facilities. In June 1998, Morse and Associates presented a draft report to the Library Executive Council. After incorporating revisions and clarifications, the Library Executive Council accepted the final report in November 1998.

The Morse Report from 1998 is a 100-page analysis based on interviews, documents, and direct observation. It has guided our safety and security planning ever since. The report makes numerous and detailed recommendations for action to improve security, from detailed technology recommendations to those directed at general policy and practice. The recommendations may be summarized here:

(1) The University of Maryland libraries have no single authority for safety and security matters. A locus of responsibility and authority for practice nevertheless must be established at the level of a director reporting directly to the dean of libraries.

(2) A wide divergence in employee attitudes exists toward safety and security, "ranging from substantial involvement to disinterest and apathy." The libraries must therefore develop an articulated philosophy along with policies and procedures, followed by a training program for all staff.

(3) An emergency response team should be formed.

(4) To accurately assess collection loss, hard data must be collected through regular, systematic, thorough inventories.

(5) Effective access-control systems and other safety and security technologies such as video cameras need to be improved for all library facilities. In this regard, several levels of technology implementation were described, but the recommendation was that at least Level 1, those recommendations having the highest priority, ought to be accomplished early on.

(6) All use of student police aides should be discontinued, and staff members themselves should assume full responsibility for safety and security in the university libraries.

This last recommendation was the most far-reaching, because it pointed in a direction that was dramatically different from existing practice. The report stated matters quite forcefully:

> The Security history of the Libraries indicates that a full-time police presence is not required, but that rapid police response must be virtually certain. The current SPA staff has no greater authority, training, or capabilities than should be provided to similar library staff. There is no reason to expect that security conditions will deteriorate. . . .
>
> The assignment of the Protection function to Library staff requires that very specific responsibilities, duties and training requirements be developed and utilized. Library personnel must be instructed regarding their responsibility to monitor their areas of responsibility and, particularly, in actions to be taken in the event of an incident.

Once the Morse Report was submitted, the libraries began to implement the recommendations, particularly those that did not require financial resources. We picked the low-hanging fruit first. Two key recommendations constituted our first priority. First, we developed a procedures manual, consolidating the former SPA manual, disparate library policies and procedures, and the security audit. The manual served as a foundation for our policy, practice, and training. New "University of Maryland Libraries Safety/Security Guidelines" were prepared in late 1998 and are mounted on the libraries' Web site, where the staff, users, faculty, students, and the public may view them. Second, the libraries discontinued the services of the SPAs. Security for McKeldin and the opening and closing of all library facilities became the responsibility of library staff. In the McKeldin Library, the circulation and information services staff bore the brunt of these changes.

To assist in the transition, the UMPD provided training in enforcing the no-food and no-drink policy, managing the exit theft–detection gates, dealing with disruptive patrons, performing opening and closing procedures, and handling medical and facilities emergencies. This training, reinforced by the new procedures manual, served as a foundation for a library-wide training effort early in 1999. Nearly 250 staff members have participated in this training, which addresses the two main objectives, that is, to ensure that staff understand security procedures and are able to implement them; and to ensure that staff are able to use techniques (such as communication or conflict-resolution skills) for dealing with problem customer situations.

Training sessions began with the discussion of a "Richter scale" instrument, one that assesses staff perceptions of the environment in which people work and the comfort level they feel while handling uncomfortable situations. Following some discussion and the application of the scale, participants received a detailed orientation, suited to their needs and responses, to the safety and security guidelines. The session ended with role-playing of various situations described in the guidelines.

In addition to the development of the procedures manual

and the training program, we began to examine the many recommendations in the Morse Report for improving security for our facilities and collections. As time passed, we allocated more fiscal resources to the effort. We invited 3M to evaluate our security gates. After their comprehensive evaluation, we invited them to present a proposal for replacing the gates with upgraded 3M models. We obtained funding through the university's enhancement fund process to replace the gates in all facilities in early 2000. Because of the closing of undergraduate library services in Hornbake Library, McKeldin Library had to expand service in the fall of 1999. With resources saved from Hornbake, we were able to upgrade video camera systems and provide card access readers to the building so that only members of the campus community with appropriate identification would have late-night access.

Once the initial staff training was completed and the manual was distributed to all staff, responsibilities for safety and security were transferred from the Public Services Division to the Planning and Administrative Services Division. The latter includes the Staff Training and Development Office, which has assumed responsibility for continued safety and security training. Conflict resolution training was offered in the summer of 2000 as part of this effort. A Safety and Security Committee—the "emergency response team" called for by the Morse Report recommendations—was also formed and charged with monitoring and improving the safety and security environment in the library, recommending training, and continually updating the procedures manual. In addition, floor marshals were identified and trained to assist in building emergencies such as fire. Floor marshals completed training that included the campus fire marshal, and the group has subsequently coordinated practice fire drills. In the summer of 1999, the members were appointed to the Safety and Security Committee. Within a year, the floor marshals had been incorporated formally into the committee's operations to ensure effective management of emergency response. It is worth mentioning that the marshals work closely with the libraries' Disaster Team, which has the primary function of responding to crises that threaten collections. The Disaster Team has had to act in at least four major "water borne" crises since August 1999, but that is another story.

We also wanted to better educate our users and to involve them in safety and security practices. In the spring of 2000, a Library Conduct Working Group was charged with reviewing our no-food and no-drink policy and making recommendations for improving communications with our users about their role as partners in the stewardship of library collections and facilities. The group submitted its report to the Library Executive Council. The recommendations were informed by contact with the university's student disciplinary system to ensure that our policy and practice were reflected campuswide.

Although much activity has taken place, one of the original goals for participating in the audit—to encourage staff involvement in and responsibility for safety and security—has remained a challenge. It is easier to write procedures and improve equipment than it is to change an organizational culture. Staff members continue to question their role and ability to handle safety and security responsibilities. Nevertheless, individuals gradually become more practiced and accustomed to dealing with these problems, and many have welcomed the authority to act. Some remain inclined to turn a blind eye to a soft drink bottle coming in the front door or to a gate alarm sounding. The anecdote at the beginning of this paper suggests how long it may take to imbue an organization with the spirit of shared responsibility in such matters.

Through continued orientation and training, as well as constant vigilance to improve our facilities and security capabilities, we remain confident that we can achieve the goal of broadly shared responsibility for safety. Although we have had what might be called "basic training," the Staff Training and Development Office has developed a training workshop that will be repeated at regular intervals, with the assistance of the UMPD. The monthly training sessions have as their goals:

(1) to promote safety and security procedures in the university libraries;

(2) to improve awareness of safety and security issues in the University of Maryland libraries and on campus;

(3) to improve interpersonal and intrapersonal skills to reduce the risk associated with difficult situations or patrons within the library system;

(4) to foster the relationship between the UMPD and the library staff;

(5) to set guidelines for conduct with regard to safety and security; and

(6) to supplement the safety and security provided to each staff member.

After completing the training session with the UMPD, members of the staff are able to meet ten behavioral objectives that ensure that baseline skills for participation in the libraries' safety and security program are met. They are able to:

(1) list the steps to identify problem situations or patrons as defined by the UMPD;

(2) state strategies that can be instituted within individual departments that would facilitate safety and security;

(3) demonstrate proper vigilance and promote sharing of information with coworkers with regard to safety and security;

(4) demonstrate constructive dialogue that promotes conflict resolution through practice sessions involving case studies;

(5) recognize members of the UMPD;

(6) recognize and follow appropriate safety guidelines provided by the UMPD;

(7) identify and record important safety information outlined by the safety and security manual;

(8) understand and practice personal safety habits;

(9) set limits for enforcing library policy, knowing when to ask for help from other staff members or to call on outside assistance; and

(10) know where emergency telephones, exits, and fire extinguishers are located within work spaces, and be able to describe their locations to others.

We continue to explore ways to test staff attitudes through focus groups and surveys. We hope these studies will yield information that will further guide our efforts to meet staff training needs in the future.

One of the Morse Report's larger recommendations remains to be addressed. The University of Maryland libraries continue to lack collection inventories. The reason for our delay in beginning this work is that we have just completed the last phase of procurement of a new library system, one with inventory capabilities far beyond our present capacity. The decision was taken with the selection of Ex Libris in late October 2000. A collection inventory can now be planned.

Finally, another of the original purposes of the Morse Report—to serve as a prototype and foundation for an ARL self-study activity—lies dormant because of lack of funding. The Association of Research Libraries remains committed to developing a generally applicable program and will seek the funding or enter into a partnership with libraries to enable it to do so. We welcome the opportunity to continue to work with ARL because we recognize the value of this experience for all of our libraries.

THE BIG PICTURE
Preservation Strategies in Context

6. Building a National Preservation Program · *National Endowment for the Humanities Support for Preservation*

Jeffrey M. Field

In a recent overview of preservation programs in the United States, Margaret Child described the development of a wide range of activities that might be called "a national preservation program." Child observed, however, that "the preservation movement . . . has been neither centralized nor systematically organized, but has instead been spontaneous, opportunistic, flexible, and multifaceted." She concluded that "if there is something that deserves to be called a 'national preservation program,' it is the totality of all the distinct and distinctive preservation activities that have developed from grassroots efforts across the country."[1] In contrast to this view, I would like to show that the framework for a national preservation program has been in place for a long time and that there has been systematic progress toward achieving two major, national goals, namely, the preservation of significant collections of source materials and the development of an infrastructure for preservation. That infrastructure must have, in turn, two components, the provision of education, training, and information services and the pursuit of research and demonstration leading to the creation of standards, best practices, and a new preservation technology.

The desire to preserve endangered books and serials has, since the 1960s, been an impetus for the formation of a national preservation plan. With support from the Council on Library Resources in 1962, Gordon Williams proposed the creation of a central preservation agency that would save an original copy of significant books.[2] The Williams Report, endorsed by the Association of Research Libraries (ARL) in 1965, was adopted as an action plan by the Library of Congress, but the Library soon found that technical, administrative, and fiscal problems inhibited its attempts to implement the plan.[3] In the early 1970s, the ARL proposed that instead of a single, national preservation collection, it would be more practical to approach the problem through the coordinated action of a number of individual research libraries.[4] Progress on this idea was delayed until the mid-1980s, when bibliographic and preservation microfilm standards and procedures had been further developed. In 1985, the Council on Library Resources issued a report that demonstrated the feasibility of undertaking a national brittle-books preservation microfilming program—a "divide and conquer" strategy that lacked only the fiscal resources necessary to undertake a national brittle-books campaign. In that same year, the National Endowment for the Humanities (NEH) established an Office of Preservation, which was charged with supporting a "sustained and coherent attack on the preservation problem."

As Margaret Child acknowledged in the examples cited in her overview, the Endowment has been, since 1979, the nation's chief source of federal support for preservation projects that have strengthened the capacity of institutions to care for their collections and preserved the content of significant humanities collections. The National Endowment for the Humanities has successfully implemented programs initially proposed in the national interest by scholarly and professional organizations, and there has been a continual broadening of the Endowment's national preservation goals to encompass the full range of the nation's cultural and research institutions in the national preservation program.

The guidelines published in 1986 for the Office of Preservation articulated the first NEH preservation mission statement: "The ability to study our cultural and intellectual heritage depends upon the availability of primary and secondary sources documenting that heritage. Vast numbers of these source documents are in imminent danger of destruction due to the disintegration of the paper on which they were printed or written or, in the case of nonprint resources, the deterioration of the medium. To ensure that the information contained in the most significant of these documents will be preserved and made available for the continuing work of scholarship in the humanities, the Endowment has established an Office of Preservation."[5]

In fact, the Endowment had provided support for brittle-books microfilming projects for several years before the formation of a special preservation office. In 1983, an NEH grant to the Research Libraries Group initiated a cooperative preservation microfilming project that became a model for the nationally coordinated brittle-books preservation microfilming program, launched by the Endowment in 1989, with the receipt of increased congressional appropriations.[6] From 1989 to the present, NEH brittle-books preservation microfilming grants have involved eighty-two institutions in projects that have preserved the intellectual content of approximately 1 million embrittled volumes, which include a large range of subjects pertaining to United States history and culture.

The United States Newspaper Program (USNP) is a second example of a systematic national effort to preserve humanities source materials. The idea for the program originated in a report on scholarly needs presented to the Endowment in 1972 by the American Council on Learned Societies. During the 1970s, NEH grants to the Organization of American Historians led to the formation of a national plan to preserve and provide bibliographic access to newspaper collections throughout the country. Launched by the Endowment in 1982, the USNP effort has now involved all the states, the District of Columbia, Puerto Rico, and the U.S. Virgin Islands in projects that have created nearly 150,000 bibliographic records for unique newspaper titles and microfilmed more than sixty million pages of deteriorating newsprint.

A third collections-focused component of the national program has involved support for the preservation of individual archival and special collections. In this area, the National Endowment for the Humanities, the Department of Education (through the former Title II-C program), the Institute of Museum and Library Services, and the National Historical Publications and Records Commission have provided discretionary federal grants for projects that have preserved hundreds of collections of textual and nontextual materials. Moreover, since 1990, NEH grants to stabilize the storage environments for material culture collections have protected twenty-nine million objects in the nation's museums and historical organizations. The inclusion of museums within its national purview further broadened the reach of the Endowment's support for preservation.

Building the infrastructure to enhance preservation practice has long been articulated as a national need. National preservation plans promoted during the 1970s stressed the need to train preservation personnel. In 1979, Paul Banks proposed the creation of a graduate program for conservators and preservation administrators. With assistance from an NEH grant, the program was initiated in 1981 at Columbia University. Its graduates have joined (or created) preservation departments at many of the nation's research libraries, and they fill other important preservation posts. With sustained NEH support since 1981, the program, now hosted by the University of Texas at Austin, continues to produce well-trained preservation professionals—a fitting memorial to its originator, who died in 2000. Through the Campbell Center for Historic Preservation Studies, George Washington University, New York University, the State University of New York at Buffalo, and the University of Delaware, NEH grants have also supported training programs for museum conservators and collections care staff.

Serving the preservation needs of research libraries has been but one aspect of the Endowment's support for preservation. In fact, that support has extended quite broadly across the country. Since 1980, when an NEH grant to the Northeast Document Conservation Center established the nation's first preservation field service program, there has been a steady increase in the geographic reach of preservation service programs. A grant in 1980 also provided support for workshops conducted by the Conservation Center for Art and Historic Artifacts in Philadelphia. In 1984, with NEH support, the Southeastern Library Network initiated a preservation service program for its eleven-state region. In 1990, the AMIGOS Bibliographic Service established a similar program for an additional five states. In 1997, the Upper Midwest Conservation Association, based in Minneapolis, established a preservation field service program, which provides surveys, workshops, disaster assistance, and information services to museums, historical organizations, libraries, and archives in the region. A sixth, Endowment-supported preservation field service program was begun in 2000 at the Balboa Art Conservation Center in San Diego, and discussions have begun regarding the formation of a program for the Pacific North-west. These projects have reached thousands of individuals, as the following statistics from the AMIGOS program demonstrate: in the ten years from its inception in 1990 to 2000, AMIGOS staff answered 9,420 telephone reference calls and, from 1996 to 2000, responded to 3,588 e-mail messages; 5,126 persons attended state, regional, and national information presentation, and, from 1993 to 2000, 3,636 persons participated in preservation and imaging workshops. In addition, fifty-three institutions benefitted from on-site surveys and preservation management consultations.

That NEH support for preservation would encompass a wide range of institutions and activities was reconfirmed in fiscal 1989, when Congress provided the Endowment with a large increase in appropriations for the Office of Preservation. Congressional interest in the national preservation program had been sparked by testimony about the brittle-books crisis presented in March 1988 by the Commission on Preservation and Access. In response, Representative Sidney Yates, chair of the Endowment's appropriations committee, asked the Endowment's chairman how much money NEH would need to solve the brittle-books problem. The chairman replied: "Your primary interest seems to be in preserving brittle books. I want to emphasize, however, that brittle books are only a part of the preservation problem. As you know, the Endowment makes awards for many other types of preservation projects . . . Any additional funds that are made available in fiscal 1989 should be used to advance the entire range of preservation activities, not just the microfilming of brittle books."[7] This statement successfully articulated the need for a broadly conceived, national preservation program, and Congress concurred.

Regional preservation service programs supported by the National Endowment for the Humanities carry out an aspect of the national preservation program that extends the reach of preservation knowledge and training to individuals in a wide variety of institutions that hold materials important for understanding local and regional history and culture. To make an even deeper impact on the ability of local institutions to care for their collections, in 2000 the Endowment initiated a new category of support for Preservation Assistance Grants (PAG), which provide up to $5,000 for training, on-site consultations, and the purchase of basic preservation supplies and equipment. In July 2000, the Endowment made 132 PAG awards to institutions in forty-one states, the District of Columbia, and Puerto Rico.

Reflecting the Endowment's service to the many audiences that benefit from the use of cultural and historical collections, NEH guidelines in use today refer to preserving resources that assist "research, education, and public programming in the humanities and that are of critical importance to our cultural heritage." During the 1990s, educators encouraged the use of primary source documents in K-12 curricula. Television documentaries, such as Ken Burns's Civil War series, have made highly visible use of manuscripts and historical photographs. Museums have a long history of interpreting primary sources for the public. Preserving humanities resources is integrally connected with enhancing teaching and learning, inside and outside the classroom.

Since 1979, our collective capacity to preserve resources has been greatly enhanced by research and demonstration projects, such as those conducted by the Image Permanence Institute (IPI) at the Rochester Institute of Technology. With NEH support since 1980, IPI projects have resulted in national standards for photographic enclosures, new techniques for enhancing the longevity of microfilm, and scientifically sound approaches to establishing proper temperature and humidity conditions for the storage of museum and library collections. Recent work by the institute on environmental conditions has incorporated the isobar concept developed in the research laboratory of the Library of Congress by Don Sebera. The Library has also, through its pursuit of mass deacidification, stimulated the private sector's development of an effective process to deacidify books and manuscripts. After twenty years of promise, the nation's research institutions finally have a dependable way to arrest the acid deterioration of paper-based materials. It is unfortunate, however, that whereas research library organizations, such as ARL and the Council on Library and Information Resources (CLIR), have persuaded the university press community to use acid-free paper in their publications, it would seem that the commercial press has not readily adopted permanent, durable paper for its output.

The preservation community is also supported by a vast and continually growing corpus of published information. In a review of preservation publications produced between 1993 and 1998, Sophia Jordan remarked that preservation has "come of age," as witnessed by the spread of preservation departments and the diversity and depth of topics covered by preservation literature. Jordan also points out that in that period, "the greatest change in the publication and dissemination of preservation literature has been the advent of the World Wide Web."[8] Numerous preservation departments and regional preservation service organizations maintain information-rich, preservation Web sites. The Council on Library and Information Resources has also been instrumental in supporting and disseminating through the Internet studies and information regarding national preservation and access issues. Moreover, the general public has been alerted about national issues in these areas through two films—*Slow Fires* and *Into the Future*—that have been broadcast on public television and widely circulated among research institutions.

Preservation is, however, but one aspect of a set of interrelated activities designed, ultimately, to increase the availability of resources for current and future use. When the Endowment made its first grants for preservation projects, it was through a program in its Research Division that also provided support to create access to collections. The creation of a separate Office of Preservation in 1985 was, at that time, a highly beneficial action that helped focus national attention on the preservation crisis. With the creation of the Division of Preservation and Access in 1992, the Endowment reintegrated these two closely related activities. In today's dynamically charged information society, the use of digital technology to enhance access to collections has become a paramount goal of research and cultural institutions, and a new set of challenges confronts the preservation community.

With skills and experience in the reformatting of fragile materials, preservation professionals are now called upon to direct digital production projects. But digitization is not yet a reliable preservation process. Advances in our capacity to ensure continuing access to digital collections will depend upon a collaboration among multiple federal agencies, the national research library organizations, and diverse knowledge domains to sustain a robust program of research and demonstration projects that will develop the standards and best practices required to certify the preservation worthiness of the new technology. Toward this end, the NEH has joined other federal agencies in support of the Digital Library Initiative—Phase II, conducted by the National Science Foundation. The Endowment's participation in the initiative ensures that projects designed to resolve the critical and distinctive issues posed by the digitization of humanities collections are included in this important national effort.

It is interesting to note that in characterizing the notion of "digital preservation," we speak or write about ensuring "continuing access to digital collections." In using this locution, we acknowledge that, with reference to digital technology, preservation and access are fused, because preservation becomes the ability over the long term to retrieve and reproduce digital information. This is why the creation of metadata standards for digital objects is such an integral part of developing a digital preservation program.

Digital technology is particularly well suited for the capture and dissemination of nontextual sources, such as photographs and audiovisual materials. As Janet Gertz has observed, "Instead of 'just' trying to solve the brittle paper problem, we now have the potential to convert other media we have avoided for many years, and to do it with a technology that users actively like."[9] But what are the best formats for audio or video longevity? Advances in these areas, particularly with respect to digital reformatting of audio and visual materials, are being developed by the Library of Congress for the operations of its new Culpeper facility.

To address the pressing need to preserve and provide access to audio recordings in the field of folklore and ethnomusicology, the American Folklife Society, with support from the National Endowment for the Humanities, convened a symposium on "Folklife Collections in Crisis" in cooperation with the American Folklife Center. The symposium took place at the Library of Congress in December 2000. We should not forget however, that there is more to learn about how best to preserve the books and serials that will continue to constitute the vast majority of holdings in research libraries. For example, when Nicholson Baker claimed that bound newspapers do not deteriorate, where was the research report to settle his claim? Abby Smith has cited a number of pressing research needs in these areas, including a study of the microclimate within a bound volume.[10]

Although drastic reductions in the Endowment's congressional appropriations since 1996 have slowed the progress of

NEH-supported preservation programs, the future will see continued NEH support for core national preservation programs, and the Endowment will continue to serve as one of the primary sources of support for projects that implement the national preservation and access agenda.

7. Safeguarding Heritage Assets

The Library of Congress Planning Framework for Preservation

 Doris A. Hamburg

A corollary goal of acquiring most cultural collections is preserving them for the future. The long-term safeguarding of the collections, or heritage assets, is most effectively accomplished through a comprehensive, systematic approach. Toward this end, the Library of Congress has identified four critical control areas—preservation, physical security, bibliographic control, and inventory control—that affect the long-term survival of the collections. Omitting or minimizing any one of these controls from the Library's activities leaves it vulnerable in meeting the needs of future users. Whereas these control areas have traditionally operated independently, overlapping concerns and approaches and the benefits of working in a more integrated manner have become clearer in the past several years as a result of developing an assessment program in each of these four areas.

This paper addresses the preservation framework being used to analyze and address the Library of Congress needs in meeting the minimum standards for safeguarding its collections from the preservation perspective, outlining the goals, methodology, and conclusions related to a preservation assessment process developed for the broad range of Library of Congress collections. Begun in 1999, the assessment process is ongoing, as new collection preservation needs are identified and others are addressed.

A difficult yet critical decision in developing the Library of Congress assessments for safeguarding its heritage assets was to acknowledge and integrate the concept that all collections are not equal. Collections and items vary with regard to intrinsic value, research value, and replacement potential. For example, Thomas Jefferson's Rough Draft of the Declaration of Independence is unique, priceless, and can never be replaced. The need to minimize any risks to this document is far greater than for a newly published book, which can easily be replaced in case of damage or loss. These risks apply to preservation, physical security, bibliographic control, and inventory control. In light of these considerations, the Library of Congress outlined five categories of value or risk in its 1997 Library of Congress Security Plan. The five levels of risk, named for metals, together form a continuum, allowing for a range of values within each category. *Platinum* is used to designate the irreplaceable items of the highest intrinsic value, such as the Rough Draft of the Declaration of Independence or Abraham Lincoln's holograph copy of the Gettysburg Address. *Gold* items are those found in special collections and have high market value and significant cultural, historical, or artifactual importance. *Silver* is the designation for collections that are at increased risk for loss because of theft, such as compact discs, comic books, videos, or training manuals or that are items that require special handling because of their condition, such as a very brittle newspapers. *Bronze* collections are served without special restrictions in the Library's reading rooms. They are identified as having relatively little or no artifactual value, and generally are replaceable. These materials may be loaned without stringent restrictions. And, finally, *copper* materials are those that the Library of Congress holds temporarily and that will not be retained over time. Using such value terminology—"gold," "silver," and so on—which is understood at all levels of the institution by staff who do or do not work with collection items, has helped to clarify discussion and identify collection needs.

Each custodial or processing division assigns the value category for each item or collection. Categorizing collections according to value is not a simple or absolute process; the methodology for doing so varies according to the type and use of the collection and in some cases according to the context of items relative to a larger group of materials held in a particular unit. Over time, one can expect that designations could change. For example, a general collection book (bronze) may become rare (gold).

In 1998, the Library established the Preservation Heritage Assets Working Group (PHAWG) to develop a preservation framework, following on the physical security framework in the 1997 Security Plan.[1] At first, the PHAWG was not certain that the framework model developed in the Security Plan to assess physical security needs would be appropriate also for preservation. Yet, upon analysis it seemed logical to build on the physical security control model, for the sake of simplicity, efficiency, feasibility, and ease of use by others already familiar with the physical security controls framework. The frameworks differ, however, in that the physical security framework includes specific actions to be taken (installation of a camera, a lock, and so on), whereas the preservation framework is broader in articulating the control measures. The preservation framework articulates an ongoing preservation effort that will never be completely finished because of the tremendous preservation needs of the collections and because of changes in the condition of objects over time.

The preservation framework formulates a comprehensive plan of minimum standards for preservation of collection materials at the Library of Congress. The framework offers an opportunity to evaluate the state of preservation throughout the Library using a Library-wide preservation assessment tool, equipped to address the range of ways that different Library custodial and processing divisions use and store their collections. Further, it fosters the integration of preservation into the broad range of activities affecting Library of Congress collections, such as acquisitions, cataloging, curatorial research, loans, use by researchers, and exhibitions.

As items or collections come into the Library, they are initially processed for bibliographic control; they may be placed in good-quality storage enclosures or conserved to provide appropriate protection for the future. This period in the life of a collection item is called the processing cycle. The items then go into the storage cycle, which becomes the long-term custodial location. Items can move in and out of the storage cycle by being moved (transit cycle) to a reading room, placed on loan, or made available for staff or researcher use (use cycle). Occasionally, an item will go on exhibition (exhibit cycle), which requires certain control measures that differ from normal use. The length of time an item is in a particular cycle varies according to the specific situation, ranging from minutes to years.

In developing the preservation control measures for each cycle and at each risk level, the most critical component was to ascertain the minimum standard needed to ensure preservation. More than the minimum can be done if desired. Minimum standards are key in developing a realistic assessment and in maintaining credibility with stakeholders and funders, who must prioritize limited resources and trust that the funds are used efficiently and effectively.

The Library's preservation framework outlines seven broad

control areas, followed by specific control measure within those areas. The seven primary areas consist of environment, emergency preparedness, storage, handling, needs assessment, physical treatment, and reformatting. The preservation control measures outline the key elements in a comprehensive preservation plan for Library collections. The control measures are accompanied by a set of definitions to ensure a universal understanding of each element. Clearly articulated specifications noted in each area facilitate communication of what is needed. For example, for a platinum item, the minimum standard for a control measure might be more stringent than for a bronze item. The plan articulates the more specific needs of each control measure as it applies to a specific value. In regulating environment, for example, tight environmental controls (Level 3, defined as "environment is controllable within tight tolerances required by special sensitive materials") apply to platinum collections. Moderate controls (Level 2, defined as "environment is controllable and generally meets specifications") are the minimum standard for gold, silver, and bronze collections. Minimal controls (Level 1, defined as "environment is controllable to a limited extent and does not generally meet specifications") apply to copper collections. Other control measures may require no differentiation according to value. For instance, the need for the development of environmental specifications exists for all collections, even if the specification is different for each value level. These are expressed on grids, easily read and understood.[2]

The control measures are preservation actions undertaken by facilities staff, librarians, readers, preservation staff, curators, and others. They indicate an approach that confirms that preservation of the collections is a collaborative effort, not limited to the staff of the Preservation Directorate. This framework emphasizes a preventive approach that involves the full range of considerations in preserving cultural collections.

For example, the way that a librarian or technician handles a book while it is being cataloged or brought to a reader for use can significantly affect the preservation of the book. Verification that maintenance is being done on the building and that appropriate levels of temperature and relative humidity are provided is important. Preventive preservation is the most cost-effective method for retaining collections over time. Once damage has occurred, it may not be fully reversible, even with the best conservation treatment. Conservation treatment is an important program element, but it is not the only one. Existing conservation treatment needs far exceed available resources to address conservation. The backlog of work needing to be done is significant. Priorities must be established. Preventing damage is by far the most logical approach for retaining collections over time.

The preservation control measures are not applicable to each cycle. Some controls, for instance, environment, apply to all cycles. Others apply as needed. As we developed our preservation framework, we decided that when an item goes for preservation treatment, it would be considered as being in the processing cycle. Therefore, most control measures apply to the processing cycle. In the storage, use, transit, and exhibit cycles, we have fewer control measures. In our preservation security framework, we created a separate grid with the relevant control measures for each of the five cycles.

Once we had developed our grids and established the minimum standards for each risk category and each cycle, we visited the custodial and processing divisions to assess the status of their preservation controls. We recognized that collaboration is crucial to our plan. With assistance from preservation staff, each division evaluated the status of preservation for each control measure. Reevaluation of the plan on a periodic basis for each division will be required. The process has been educational for all who participated and is seen as a positive tool, drawing attention to problem preservation areas and previously unidentified concerns.

Preservation staff members learned from each division about collection use, value, and preservation needs. The assessment process has created a broader understanding among librarians of the elements involved in preserving the collections. To achieve this, a grid identifying each control measure was marked in terms of each control element's completion status: C: Completed; P: Partially completed; U: Unmet; H: In-House (with existing funds from within the unit); F: Funded; and NA: Not Applicable. The evaluation was generally broad, because the assessment focused on collections rather than individual items. A future project will be to return to specific collections within a division to identify their unmet control measures.

The development of the physical security, preservation, bibliographic, and inventory frameworks has led to increased integration of effort and understanding of the interrelated goals of these four areas in safeguarding the Library's assets. For example, as we surveyed the collections for physical security needs, we were able to clarify the requirement for enhanced or new vault spaces. Preservation teamed up with security staff to have some of the vaults built with an environmental component, so that the vault would provide temperatures at a set point in the fifty-to-fifty-five-degree Fahrenheit range. Reducing the storage environment temperature from the average room temperature of about seventy-two degrees to fifty degrees can extend the life expectancy of the collections from as much as fivefold to sixfold. For the transit cycle, the development of new book carts addressed both preservation and physical security concerns. Integrating the physical security and preservation elements yields cost benefits, when managers collaborate to solve overlapping concerns.

In our assessment for each control measure in the five cycles, we built a database that has proved invaluable. The database, using Microsoft ACCESS™, helps us manage, use, maintain, and update the data. The database allows us to perform statistical calculations and analysis of the data for all the divisions involved, so that we can review and discuss the information obtained. The Library has made its statistical reports available by value category (platinum, gold, and so on); cycle (such as process, use, or transit); division; completion status (control measures completed, unmet, and so on); and individual preservation control measure element (environment, emergency preparedness, and the rest). Reports can be generated across divisions or for one division only. The database provides an assessment for a particular control measure across all divisions, giving us a focus for shared problems and successes. We can group issues where there are shared problems, which facilitates collaborative solutions, reducing costs over the long term.

The preservation assessment framework has yielded a number of benefits. Standardization of terms enhances communication in the pursuit of safeguarding heritage assets. Assessment and analysis articulate a long-term preservation picture for the institution. By quantifying the preservation status and needs of the Library's collections, we can develop a plan for action. Through periodic reassessment, we can track and demonstrate progress in a quantifiable manner. The Library will work toward grouping similar preservation projects across the institution to enhance efficiency and reduce costs.

8. Taking Care · *An Informed Approach to Library Preservation*

 Jan Merrill-Oldham

The burgeoning of information resources in electronic form, created and distributed worldwide, has had a profound methodological, organizational, and financial impact on the research enterprise. Today, the users of any large academic library expect organized access to vast numbers of electronic journals, books, works of art, and databases, as well as the equipment required for viewing, printing, downloading, and manipulating them. The cost of licensing and purchasing electronic publications of enduring value, and of the hardware, software, and technical expertise required to deliver them, is steep. And even as communications technologies are transformed by leaps and bounds, the flow of paper, film, magnetic tape, and discs into traditional library collections continues unceasingly.

The dawn of a new and volatile information environment —an environment that will surely change in ways that cannot yet be predicted—raises questions about the ability of institutions to embrace and manage an ever-broadening range of services and stewardship responsibilities. As a growing body of information is distributed over networks, concerns are inevitably raised regarding the bibliographic, reference, and instructional attention being deflected from collections of books, papers, and other materials amassed over the course of centuries. It is not clear how we will fund the costly systems that will be required to provide sustained access to electronic resources and simultaneously find the means to do the same for traditional collections. There is nothing new about complexity and competition for dollars in libraries, but the stakes are being raised.

In order to be effective advocates for the care and long-term preservation of library collections, we must cultivate a stronger and more focused message regarding the role of preservation programs in a modern information environment. We are well equipped to do so. Over the course of the past thirty years, we have learned and confirmed much about the physical nature and aging characteristics of library materials, what strategies are most effective for extending their useful lives, and how to apply these in cost-effective ways. Following is a review of the preservation tools with which we must continue to work effectively: environmental control, emergency preparedness and response, collections care and handling, conservation, commercial binding, and reformatting. What strategies have been successful and are well worth championing in a new information age that also carries with it most of the technologies of the past?

We have been hearing for decades that controlling environmental conditions is the single most important action that a library can take to ensure a long life for collections of all types. The aging of books, papers, photographs, film, magnetic tape, and discs is inextricably linked to the conditions under which they are stored. In general, an environment that promotes the longevity of organic materials is characterized by cold, dry air that is free from gaseous and particulate pollutants. Light is filtered to screen out ultraviolet radiation and is controlled for intensity and duration. Furnishings and surface finishes are composed of materials that are free from harmful gas emissions.

In recent years, many of the world's oldest and largest libraries have upgraded environmental systems in existing buildings and have constructed new libraries and storage facilities designed to promote the preservation of their collections. The development and maintenance of hospitable environmental conditions is a truly strategic act, affecting materials collectively rather than selectively. Also strategic are such building routines as rigorous testing, maintenance, and replacement of pumps, motors, and fans; changing of air filters; integrated pest management; regular cleaning of floors and other surfaces; and skilled vacuuming of collections.

Alongside requests for expanded technical capabilities and increased collections purchasing power, funds for environmental management must appear predictably and persistently in every annual budget proposal. We cannot allow the need for ongoing maintenance and physical improvements to slip off the radar screen as pressure to offer distance learning and other important new services mounts. Paper- and plastics-based collections will not disappear as electronic sources become more prominent, nor will our responsibility to provide safe housing for them.

If a high-quality off-site storage facility is part of the library's strategy for managing ever-expanding holdings, take full advantage of the options that cool, orderly, secure storage presents for establishing truly rational preservation priorities. Never before have we had so good an opportunity to invest typically lean preservation resources in those holdings that are at greatest risk of being lost if they are not conserved or copied promptly. Storage at fifty degrees Fahrenheit and 35 percent relative humidity slows down the aging process enough to truly legitimize long-range preservation planning. The power of integrated library systems can also be brought to bear on the highly systematic development and implementation of preservation priorities. If the incidence of damage and embrittlement can be recorded, for example, either as materials are transferred to storage or are circulated from it, it will be possible to address preservation problems in a meaningful sequence, however slowly.

Like environmental control, emergency preparedness and response support and legitimize all other preservation activity. Although many institutions have put disaster preparedness plans into place, few go far enough in their efforts to prepare for incidents that could result in major loss. We must be more organized in our efforts to train an adequate number of staff to respond to collections emergencies large and small in a deliberate and informed way. Responsibilities should be built into job descriptions rather than left to personal preference and chance. Staff with diverse skills and experience must be involved in emergency readiness to ensure that a range of talents can be mobilized when they are needed. Too much homogeneity strips the library of its ability to manage an emergency skillfully when a conference calls away too many members of the disaster team.

Well-stocked emergency supply closets that include such tools as water vacuums, dehumidifiers, fans, and extension cords are a high priority. Experience has shown that access to the tools needed in a library emergency must be restricted. Flashlights, plastic sheeting, and other supplies are mysteriously attractive and can dwindle if they are not kept under lock and key, hampering the first hours of a cleanup effort. Emergency power-generating capacity should be reviewed throughout the library system and improved where necessary, even if it takes time and a concerted effort to analyze systemwide needs, set priorities, and move adequate funding into place.

Be certain that the emergency support systems needed at 2:00 A.M. on a Saturday morning can really be mobilized and that every important vendor is called periodically to ensure that companies are still in business and telephone numbers are still working. Be sure that there are multiple options available for securing freezer space for wet library materials, and plan to use a disaster recovery vendor for freezing rather than a firm whose main job it is to store and distribute the public food supply.

Finally, staff must have time to read the library emergency preparedness and response literature, to assign roles and responsibilities, to create documentation specific to the local situation, and to organize and participate in emergency training programs and exercises. While no degree of preparation suffices in certain situations, many collections emergencies involving water can result in minimal loss if they are managed by a trained response team.

Cultivating an environment for library collections care and handling that promotes longevity requires observation, analysis, planning, and a commitment of resources. Guidelines for storing and using library collections have appeared repeatedly in the literature, and although such prescriptions may be shopworn, they remain important blueprints for action. The job of communicating good care and handling practices to library staff and users is difficult to manage convincingly. Signs, exhibits, news articles, and Web sites can trivialize the issues or be effective consciousness-raising tools, depending on how ideas are expressed. Seek tough criticism when creating educational products for staff and users. Remember that messages gradually become invisible in a familiar landscape and must be refreshed. Goals for an education program are various because of the many material types that a research library collects and preserves, but the overarching one is to get as many users as possible to buy into the principle of the public good. Library resources must be cared for and protected by the entire user community on behalf of the community.

The way that collections are treated in public areas suggests their ultimate fate. We can choose to let books and journals pile up on floors around copy machines, or we can provide book trucks for materials awaiting return to the stacks. We can opt for the convenience of book drops, or take the extra care required for human intervention. The politics of closing book drops is dicey, but the argument against them can be made in compelling ways. Over-the-counter returns coupled with good staff training can have significant long-term benefits.

We must communicate regularly with vendors and manufacturers to ensure that fast-disappearing right-angle book copiers are carried forward into the digital age, and we must continue to encourage people to copy pages one at a time, at least when to do otherwise would be to ruin a volume. Microfilm readers, videocassette recorders, and other readers and playback equipment should be kept as clean as possible to avoid the transfer of dirt from machine to medium. Budgets may not support an optimal level of care, but it is important to allocate reasonable resources to machine maintenance to help minimize the damage that media can sustain during reading and playback. We must reconsider once again the ways in which the stacks are managed, and whether they might be kept cleaner. Cyclical vacuuming is an effective way to reduce abrasive dirt and grit and the damaging moisture that can be trapped around books and papers by blankets of dust. While a full collections vacuuming cycle may not be completed for years, it ensures that there is continual improvement in the condition of the stacks and that there is a mechanism in place for dealing with trouble spots.

Regarding processing, it is important to foster an environment in which all materials are handled consistently, according to an established protocol, from the time they enter the acquisitions workflow. Materials check-in, temporary storage, cataloging, and end-processing are among the junctures at which handling decisions can affect permanently the condition of a library collection. Procedures that promote longevity are often as straightforward as ensuring that books do not lean on shelves and that compact discs are rehoused in jewel cases. Regarding processing supplies, care must be exercised in making selections. Acidic pamphlet binders, for example, can still be purchased through standard library supply catalogs and obviously should be avoided.

End-processing is a point at which the library's security program can get a big boost. Although bookplates are an elegant vehicle for acknowledging ownership, edge stamping is a more aggressive way to mark an object as library property and therein to make it a less desirable object of theft. Edge stamps are easily seen signs of ownership and are hard to eradicate. They lower the value of an object, often significantly, thus providing some protection against resale.

Regarding the decades-long debate over whether to mark items in special collections, the guidelines that have been developed by the Rare Book and Manuscript Section of the American Library Association's Association of College and Research Libraries provide a structure within which a variety of approaches can be considered. In general, libraries must navigate conflicting needs and goals, caught between the desire to preserve value and aesthetic characteristics and the need to prevent accidental and intentional loss. For general collections, electronic library security systems, while not foolproof, are effective deterrents to theft, particularly when security devices are inserted in all circulating materials.

Despite our best efforts, damage to library materials is unavoidable and likely to be widespread, and thus conservation must be a priority. A great deal of attention was devoted during the 1980s and 1990s to the development of methods and work flows for carrying out high-quality book repair for circulating collections. Likewise, the conservation of materials in special collections has evolved considerably in recent decades, with conservation treatments tending to be less invasive and more likely to retain evidence of original intention whenever possible. Methods and mending materials are chosen for their chemical, mechanical, and structural advantages; and in the case of general collections, work is done in batches to increase productivity. Custom-fitted boxes are constructed to protect library materials from light, dust, and handling and to substitute for treatment when the workload is overwhelming.

Significant space is required to manage an effective collections conservation program for research library materials. The larger the collection, the more tending—and therefore the more square footage—its care will require. Ideally, every item that circulates and is returned to the library in damaged condition will be repaired before it is sent back to the shelf. Programs must be balanced so that the more important bindings are saved through conservation and other materials are commercially rebound. There is an inevitable gap, however, between the amount of repair and rebinding required for a circulating collection and the work to which a library can afford to commit. Setting priorities is no easy task, even if a library chooses to concentrate almost exclusively on the treatment of materials that are heavily used.

Certain classes of damaged materials must be earmarked for rapid turnaround, and in such cases, the repair team must deliver services that demand skill and speed. When a damaged reference book leaves the shelf one day and is repaired and put back in use the next, the conservation program can be judged a success. For all but the most pressing needs, however, repair problems in most institutions often go unaddressed, and the condition of collections tends to worsen significantly as the collections age. We have not yet made the case successfully to funders that library holdings require significant upkeep. As a result, resources for collections maintenance are lean. If salaries for skilled conservation staff and a suitable work space are beyond reach, commercial binding is an option. Although instructions for carrying out basic treatment procedures are documented in several important publications, it nonetheless makes little sense to proceed with an in-house treatment program if the program cannot be staffed adequately. It is easy for the preservation unit to become a black hole into which damaged materials pour and from which little emerges.

This is not to paint a gloomy picture of the state and practice of conservation in libraries. Today we understand the nature and behavior of the kinds of materials that we collect even better than we did only a decade ago, and research in conservation science is ongoing. More staff members in research libraries are dedicated to collections treatment than ever before, and more practitioners recognize the need to expand and strengthen these efforts. More conservation positions are migrating to the permanent ranks, and more are recognized as part the professional workforce.

For general collections, goals are generally similar across institutions. In special collections, however, to treat the letters and poems of Emily Dickinson, the page proofs of James Joyce's *Ulysses,* or the globes of Gerardus Mercator requires consummate skill. We know that objects ultimately deteriorate, but uninformed conservation treatment can do far more damage to library materials than time and wear. We must ensure that the conservators of rare books, manuscripts, photographs, and other unique and important objects have at their command years of training, ample technology, established channels of communication with knowledgeable curators, the time to research unknown objects, and generous opportunities for continuing education.

In the absence of access to trained conservators, in-house treatment of special collections begins and ends with proper housing. If resources allow, conservation treatments are contracted out. Neither a sizable professional staff, however, nor a generous budget for contract work eases the difficulty of setting conservation priorities. The gap between need and capacity is simply overwhelming.

One viable approach to setting conservation priorities for special collections is to focus on minor treatment, with the goal of maximizing the number of items restored to good condition. Another is to treat damaged materials that scholars are slated to use in the coming year. Planned classroom use can be an important criterion upon which to base treatment priorities, as can exhibition requirements. Although the conservation of materials for the purpose of display is sometimes viewed as a deterrent to accomplishing more systematic goals, scholarly exhibits naturally highlight significant works and can be as good a strategy as any for establishing goals. Yet another approach is to focus on major treatment of a few great treasures each year—objects of indisputable and enduring importance.

Institutions can sometimes pursue multiple treatment strategies, but every choice requires careful consideration, and every treatment will be undertaken at the expense of another. Special collections conservation is a compelling enterprise, however, and its potential for attracting new funds should not be overlooked.

Few institutions can keep up with the need to repair books in circulating collections in particular, and the importance of commercial binding services for modern general collections is widely recognized. Managing a binding program is not as straightforward as it may appear to those who have never been involved in the decision making and preparation process. The way a volume is bound dictates to a great extent whether it will open well, will be able to withstand repeated photocopying, and will retain most of its original features after binding. Bindery preparation staff must also be able to assess book structure, the condition of paper, and the way that these features influence the development of a binding specification. Staff members should have the opportunity not only to develop basic skills but also to master the more sophisticated aspects of binding that result in a better outcome.

Often discussed are methods for dealing with paperback volumes when the budget is not adequate to fund comprehensive binding. It may be better to commercially bind paperbacks selectively based on patterns of use than to employ in-house binding techniques that work in the short term but cause damage and failure in the long term. If budgets will not stretch to accommodate needs, journals must take first priority and monographs that have truly become unusable, second. The efficacy of early intervention, and the difficulty and cost of delayed binding, argue for a prompt response to binding needs.

Among the most daunting of challenges for research libraries is the mandate to retain a large part of their collections "permanently," a challenge that can be met through reformatting. Although the job of managing materials while they are being processed is a logistical puzzle, it pales beside the difficulty of monitoring and managing ongoing preservation needs once materials are absorbed into the collections. Looking across rows of deteriorating nineteenth-century books, or boxes of important nineteenth-century papers that have become brittle, it is hard to imagine how we will grapple with physical problems that are too massive to solve exhaustively. Certain modern materials decay so rapidly that we have not yet formulated a response to their physical problems, let alone resolved them.

By way of example, many of the papers that record the work of great thinkers can no longer be manipulated without damaging them each time they are handled. Some collections are huge, and most are made up of items that have considerably more value in the aggregate than as discrete objects. Preservation surrogates allow us to depend less on failing paper. They ensure that intellectual access persists and, in the case of microfilm, serve as a platform for making new microform, paper, or electronic copies on demand. Microfilm can be exploited as a source for new versions, and at the same time it promises hundreds of years of reliable access to the master copy. There have never been large budgets for copying deteriorated materials, and with every passing year preservation resources must stretch further. Nonetheless, libraries continue to identify and copy aging collections of significance, and a segment of our holdings could potentially survive for a very long time.

Fundamental to the microfilming process are both strict adherence to national standards and unrelenting quality control. These goals apply whether film has been created in-house or by a commercial service. Image capture must be of consistently high quality if it is to serve as a permanent record of the original work or as a platform for making digital copies. Unless paper is so brittle that it fractures with gentle handling, we can retain original copies of reformatted materials for consultation until they are no longer able to serve a useful purpose.

When making film, the printing negative is all-important. In addition to protecting the master negative from damage, it is the source from which the use copy is produced. That copy can be created on film, paper, or as an electronic resource. Regarding bibliographic control, there is no point in expending resources to reproduce a text if readers cannot discover it easily. There are untold numbers of aging pamphlets in the stacks of some of our oldest libraries, for example, that will become known to scholars for the first time as we clean up or create cataloging records during reformatting projects. Our international system for preserving and distributing fragile and rarely held titles depends upon identifying and describing materials accurately and noting missing issues and other anomalies.

Modern materials such as videotapes, many types of sound recordings, nitrate negatives, and CD-ROMs (compact discs with read-only memory) have begun to present us with an overwhelming array of physical and management challenges. Sound and video recordings, for example, have an unpredictable shelf life, are costly to copy, and, unlike a microfilmed book, will need to be copied repeatedly over the years if they are to survive. Currently, the average cost to remaster one hour of video play time is approximately two hundred dollars plus materials.

Copyright permissions present vexing issues in preservation, for we must be able to migrate short-lived forms of information long before they are in the public domain. To preserve some materials will require that we secure preservation privileges that we currently do not have. Furthermore, preservation reformatting promises to be expensive, and we are unlikely to be able to do very much of it. It is hard to imagine that we will find the means to support conversion and maintenance of any significant percentage of our nonprint resources if current costs and the legal environment remain unchanged. And it will be many decades before we begin to realize the impact of the resulting losses on our intellectual life.

The electronic environment promises to provide new and sometimes better ways to preserve information, provided that we are able to devise strategies that guarantee the persistence of electronic files into the indefinite future. Digital copying, if executed expertly, eliminates the gradual degradation of text, images, and sound that characterizes analog reproductions. New frontiers are opening before us that only a short time ago seemed remote and improbable. Consider, by way of example, the revisiting of history through early photographs. The daguerreotypes held in fourteen repositories at Harvard are a useful case in point. These images are among the earliest ever captured by photographic means and are of great value to scholars and researchers in many fields Until recently, they could be accessed only by the Harvard community and visitors to the collections in Harvard's libraries and museums. Because of their delicacy, fragility, and uniqueness, the daguerreotypes could be consulted only a few at a time and could not be borrowed for research purposes, however compelling. Repeated handling threatened glass and seals and generally increased the exposure of the unique, silver-coated copper plates to risk.

Comprehensive photographing and subsequent digitizing of every known daguerreotype in Harvard's libraries and museums have addressed the problem of access and created unprecedented opportunities for study and research. Copying and online display are creating new audiences for Harvard's early photographs, making images widely available for examination, comparison, and use in new ways.

Electronic reproductions are no substitute for the real thing when it comes to experiencing history firsthand, but they fulfill most purposes admirably and open up brand new avenues for exploration. The conversion of traditional library resources to more convenient, and sometimes more functional, electronic files is an attractive option for everything from movies and news broadcasts to newspapers and science treatises. It is practical, however, only in cases where materials merit the cost of creating, maintaining, and migrating digital files to ever newer forms, and where adequate funds are available to do so.

The delivery of searchable texts over networks is rapidly becoming a mainstream approach to publishing, much to the satisfaction of those readers who are fortunate enough to have access to fast networks and unlimited printing. The convenience and power of electronic texts and images prompt us to wonder what place paper, film, discs, and other physical instances of information resources will have in tomorrow's publishing world, what will replace them, and to what extent we will backtrack to capture existing resources in new forms. In the preservation arena, to make, store, and deliver microfilm costs a small fraction of what it costs to scan and process an electronic text. It seems likely that we will proceed on multiple tracks, taking advantage of existing copying techniques for some classes of material and pursuing more expensive, more flexible forms of access for others. The beauty of film is that it addresses preservation problems relatively inexpensively and can serve as source material for creating digital access should that prove desirable at any time.

Over the coming decades, digital table of contents projects will rescue unindexed serial runs from neglect. Existing finding aids will be converted from paper to machine-readable form, and new and important indexes and finding aids will be created. Large numbers of visual resources will be made available electronically and used as never before. Historic scores, essays, and logbooks will blend with modern demographic and economic data to create altogether new relationships. And as texts and indexes are recycled for new uses, some will at the same time also be preserved.

We have difficult choices before us regarding what information to gather and what to save for the long term, as has been the case since we first began to collect, organize, and store information, and these choices will be greatly complicated by the fact that modern documents need never be finished—no version need be finalized. Despite logistical, financial, and legal issues, however, we will build digital collections that are critical for teaching and research, and we will use them in harmony with information resources in many other forms. We will preserve materials at great risk of being lost forever and imbue them with new power. We will rescue films and databases, ephemera, and great works.

In contemplating these possibilities, libraries, library users, and society at large must come to grips with major financial needs and how they might better be met. We must do more to raise awareness regarding the fragile nature of library resources, ancient and modern, and to stimulate public interest in their survival. We must build on our successes to make a stronger case to federal and state governments, to major funding sources, and to the community at large for ongoing support. The forging of connections between the past and the present, and between our accomplishments and our aspirations, is, after all, a large part of what it means to be human.

THE SILVER LINING
Coping with Theft, Vandalism, Deterioration, and Bad Press

9. **Picking Up the Pieces** · *The Lengthy Saga of a Library Theft*

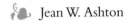 Jean W. Ashton

On July 5, 1994, the Tuesday following Independence Day weekend, Consuelo Dutschke, a curator who had been engaged in cataloging Columbia University's Rare Book and Manuscript Library's collection of medieval and Renaissance manuscripts, went into the secured vault of the closed stacks to consult Western MS 29, a codex she had been working on several weeks before. To her surprise, although the preservation case was on the shelf in its proper place, the box was empty. After a few moments of conversation with other senior staff members to make sure that the manuscript had not been removed for some legitimate reason, she came into my office with two colleagues to report that we apparently had a major problem. A cursory shelf check had revealed that in addition to Western MS 29, several other manuscripts usually housed on adjacent shelves were also missing from their cases, including at least two that had been examined by readers and reshelved by staff in early June.

Although we sensed that something unusual was happening, I decided to delay mentioning Consuelo's discovery to the staff as a whole until after we had gathered more information. While the three curators, joined by the remaining member of the internal administrative staff, began to read the Medieval-Renaissance shelves, card catalogs in hand, I went down to the Columbia University libraries administrative office to alert the university librarian to the possibility of a serious theft.

More than six years later, the consequences of this theft of what eventually turned out to be $1.3 million worth of books and manuscripts were still with us. We suffered a severe loss: some of our materials were still missing, and many could not be recovered intact because they had been mutilated. Moreover, efforts to deal with the crime and its prolonged aftermath were time consuming and upsetting for the staff. Nonetheless, by now we are able to see some positive effects from what was a profoundly negative experience.

First, thanks to the hard work of the Federal Bureau of Investigation (FBI), the New York City Police Department, the U.S. Attorney's office, and the international community of booksellers and manuscript dealers, the thief was apprehended, sentenced, and removed from his chosen sphere of criminal activity for a number of years.[1] Second, issues relating to the safety of library materials temporarily assumed a greater importance on the campus than had been the case before, resulting in the installation of an electronic security system in the Rare Book and Manuscript Library, the establishment of a standing committee to deal with general collection loss, reexamination of insurance practices, and better communications between librarians and the university's legal and security staffs. Finally, a landmark opinion from the federal judge, Lewis A. Kaplan, who presided over the sentencing hearing, articulated with great clarity to the public at large the serious implications of the theft of cultural materials. We understand that his decision to depart upward from the recommended sentencing guidelines has had a measurable impact on courts across the county. I hope, in the brief paragraphs that follow, both to tell the story of the *United States v. Daniel Spiegelman* and to offer some comments that may serve to guide others who may find themselves in similar situations.[2]

Within an hour of the discovery that Western MS 29 was missing from the shelf, the associate librarian was in contact with the Columbia University security office, the 26th Precinct of the New York City Police Department, and, shortly thereafter, the regional office of the FBI. Fortunately—or rather, unfortunately—the Columbia libraries had been victim of two thefts of restricted materials in the five years preceding 1994 (although quite different ones and on a much smaller scale), and we thus had some idea of the protocols and procedures to be followed. My own experiences at the New-York Historical Society, where I had been librarian before coming to Columbia in 1993, had also made me particularly aware of the institutional sensitivities that could make legal action difficult if the issue was not handled quickly and carefully. The Blumberg case, with its disappointing outcome for libraries, had only recently been settled.[3] It was therefore gratifying to see that Columbia's librarian had no hesitation in urging us to make sure that the crime was reported and that the relevant Association of College and Research Libraries (ACRL) procedural guidelines be followed to the letter.

As soon as the inventory was finished, a list of the fourteen missing medieval codices and fragments and the eight Arabic manuscripts that had disappeared from an adjacent shelf was compiled and sent to our contacts in the rather tight community of dealers and scholars who might be likely to come across such items or happen upon them in the market. Within a few days, we had refined and amplified the list by adding what secondary cataloging information we had in our files along with, in some cases, photographs or photocopies. We made sure that the Antiquarian Booksellers' Association of

America, the International Foundation for Art Research, and the relevant professional e-mail lists that we subscribed to also had copies of the list. I think it safe to say that within two weeks, most of the scholarly world interested in such things knew as much about the Columbia losses as we did.

As might be expected, the internal consequences of our theft were distressing and unpleasant. Members of the staff were fingerprinted and questioned; lists of former employees were compiled and reviewed; security and lock-up practices were subjected to scrutiny. For months, insurance adjusters, law enforcement officials from a variety of units, and university administrators were likely to show up at any time of the day for tours of the restricted areas. Registration logs were examined, locks were changed, and keys were confiscated. Personnel practices, which had been fairly strict to begin with, were tightened so that no staff member was permitted in the stacks alone. Everyone was a potential suspect. Although the tension eased after a while as the day-to-day work of the library resumed, it was only after the thief was identified and caught, and his means of egress reported, that people were entirely confident that they or their colleagues had not been in some way responsible for the loss.

Reconciling the need to get full information to the book community with administrative pressure to maintain institutional privacy presented a major problem that also affected the staff. Some alumni, donors, and faculty members were upset and were filled with unfounded suspicions when news of the theft reached them. Others were even more upset when they felt they were not being fully informed. The need to monitor the general flow of information about the theft kept everyone on edge. Although the university's public information office was responsible for press relations, reporters were likely to call librarians or faculty members directly, and it was hard not to blurt out some comment that might mislead the public or hinder the investigation. Even after the suspect was arrested, great care had to be taken not to say or do something that might jeopardize the Columbia case.

Throughout 1994 and early 1995, we worked closely with the detective from the local precinct and with the special agent from the FBI. Several promising leads turned out to be useless, and on one occasion a "sting" operation that had been set up and involved crossing state lines failed at the last minute because of some confusion about the appraised value of the particular items involved. Empty manuscript boxes were found in another area of the rare book stacks on a different floor, but because we did not think the two disappearances were related, we found it particularly painful to report the second, because it was beginning to seem even to us as if we had completely lost control of the collections.

Late in the spring of 1995, to our relief, I began to get telephone calls from a series of highly reputable manuscript dealers in Western Europe—from Switzerland, France, Germany, and the Netherlands—reporting that a young man who apparently had several pseudonyms had shown them pictures or given them descriptions of items that corresponded to items on our list. Finally, in June 1995, Sebastiaan S. Hesselink, the owner of Antiquariaat FORUM in Utrecht, called me on a Wednesday to report that a customer had brought him a picture and description of a manuscript of the *Roman de la Rose* that he recognized from the Columbia list. I notified the FBI, which was able to mobilize Interpol in time to arrest Daniel Spiegelman the following afternoon when he returned to the shop, manuscript in hand. The arrest was reported by the Associated Press and the *New York Times* on June 17, 1995.

But the story was far from over. Daniel Spiegelman, who had in his possession several Columbia identification cards, issued under a variety of names, as well as dealer catalogs and information files, was not, as we had wrongly suspected, a student or rare book specialist. Rather, he was a felon who had served time in a federal institution on forgery charges some years earlier. Sensitized by his unpleasant experience in an American jail, he fought hard against the prospect of extradition to the United States. According to later stories in the Dutch newspapers, he had tried to commit suicide on the way to jail when he was arrested. When a detailed plan of escape was thwarted, he was put into a high-security facility. Eventually, in an apparent attempt to gain clemency by trading information, he revealed to investigators in the Netherlands that he had several caches of stolen items hidden in New York.

We were appalled to discover that the scope of Spiegelman's theft was so broad. We had focused on the medieval and Arabic items, which had been stored in a single location. Now, materials turned up in his storage boxes and in the photographs found in his possession that we had not known were missing: 237 maps from a very rare German edition of the 1667 Blaue atlas that had been extra-illustrated by an illustrious Columbia alumnus in the early nineteenth century with his own collection of early maps and charts and had been on display only a few months earlier; miscellaneous medieval and early modern indentures; presidential and early Federal period letters, including a note from George Washington to John Jay on the occasion of the first session of the first meeting of the Supreme Court; and stock certificates from Thomas Edison's early business ventures. We felt as if we had discovered the theft all over again and felt doubly vulnerable at the evidence that he had razored materials out of bound volumes and penetrated deep into drawers and boxes of material that were in the midst of files or document cases used only by specialized researchers. It took us more than six months to gather accurate information about the missing materials and to confirm ownership of them in a way that would satisfy the law enforcement authorities and the courts.

Despite the efforts of the accused thief and his attorneys, extradition papers were prepared for submission in the beginning of December 1995. At Columbia, because the counsel's office had no one assigned to the case, we were dependent on calls from the police or the FBI for information about what was going on. Suddenly, on the last business day of the year, a television news station in Oklahoma telephoned the Rare Book and Manuscript Library to ask for comment on a story that had appeared that day in the Dutch press: Daniel Spiegelman's lawyer claimed that an American embassy official had revealed that the FBI was investigating a possible link between his client and the Oklahoma City bombing the previous April.

The FBI denied the allegation, but the most sensational of the Amsterdam papers gave it full coverage. A published photograph of Spiegelman, described as a suspected American terrorist, was accompanied by the familiar image of smoke and burning buildings. Releasing the story was, so we were led to believe, a ploy by Spiegelman's attorney to buy time, because the Dutch will not extradite anyone who might be accused of a capital crime in his or her home country. It was a pretty spectacular form of defense, and it succeeded. No connection between the accused and the bombings was established, but the extradition was delayed for twelve months. Spiegelman was not returned to New York until December 1996, a year and a half after his arrest.

In April 1997, after being indicted for the theft of $1.3 million worth of books and manuscripts from Columbia (along with additional charges relating to the transport of weapons across state lines and a forged passport), Daniel Spiegelman entered into a plea agreement with the U.S. Attorney. He did not reveal the location of any stolen material that had not at that time been returned, but we were finally given some clue as to how he had stolen the items in the first place. For various reasons, information could not be freely shared by the law enforcement agencies, but we have surmised and now believe that he shinnied up an unused dumbwaiter shaft that extended from a public area of the general stacks to the rare book floor and had used tools to dismantle existing walls, reassembling them when he was through (something that is no longer possible because of building renovation).

He had made multiple visits to the stacks at night when the Rare Book and Manuscript Library, on the top floor of the massive Butler Library, was closed. By careful selection of materials that were not likely to be in daily use or that were stored in files and drawers where their loss would not be easily visible, he had covered his traces successfully for several months. Because the items were not tagged with electronic tape, he could leave the building easily without alerting the security guard. The library's (now abandoned) custom of storing duplicates of exhibition labels and catalog entries in the preservation boxes had provided him with the information needed to sell his harvest. At the time of his arrest, approximately one-quarter of the stolen items, including more than two hundred maps from the nine-volume Blaue atlas, were still missing.

A parole officer assigned by Judge Lewis Kaplan to prepare a report to aid in sentencing contacted Columbia for information in May 1997. It was at this point that we decided to use the powers of the law to force some good from what had been a thoroughly unpleasant experience. Susan Galligan, a Columbia attorney, worked with me to produce a letter for the court, in which we argued that consideration should be given to the nature of the offense: seven-hundred-year-old manuscripts and early maps were not the same as fur coats or cash; they were cultural materials representing our shared heritage. Moreover, they had been placed in libraries as a public trust so that they would be available to generations of scholars in the context of other scholarly materials. Somewhat to our surprise, the judge agreed. At the sentencing hearing in June, Judge Kaplan announced his intention to depart upward from the newly adopted federal sentencing guidelines, which would have allowed a sentence of no more than thirty-seven months. By this time, Spiegelman had spent approximately twenty-four months in custody.

The defense objected. Judge Kaplan gave Spiegelman time to make his case, but also instructed the U.S. Attorney's office to assist Columbia if it should prove to be necessary. After a vain attempt to find manuscript dealers who would agree to argue in court that the "cultural value" argument was irrelevant, that is, that market value was the sole determinant of worth, the defense lawyers asked for a public hearing. For that hearing, they wrote a letter to the judge enumerating points that they felt invalidated the Columbia position, that is, they argued that the existence of photocopies made protection of originals unimportant; that the thousands of surviving manuscripts made the disappearance of single ones trivial; that incunabula often existed in multiple identical copies; and that librarians were not, in any case, adequate appraisers of value.

We responded by asking a group of scholars who had worked on similar materials, including such well-known writers as Simon Schama and Robert Darnton, to agree to testify about the importance of original documents of the kind that had been stolen. David Kastan, a Shakespearean scholar, was perhaps the most eloquent: materials such as these, he argued, form the substance of history that has not yet been written.

The experts ultimately were allowed to submit their comments in writing instead of making a court appearance, but at the hearing held on March 20, 1998, I was called to the stand to testify in person. Using actual books and maps, including some of the recovered items, I spent more than three hours demonstrating to the court the difference between originals and copies and explaining the nature of artifactual evidence. When the defense objected to the participation of the Assistant U.S. Attorney in the hearing, Judge Kaplan himself stepped down from the bench and donned white gloves to examine items that had been found in Spiegelman's possession, including the note from George Washington to John Jay and a seventeen-foot-long vellum chronicle of the history of the kings of France.

On April 24, 1998, Judge Kaplan issued a thirty-seven-page opinion sentencing Spiegelman to sixty months in federal custody, a restitution fee for the unrecovered items, and a three-year period of probation. Although many of our maps and manuscripts are still missing, Judge Kaplan's eloquently argued statement has had, we understand, an impact on the conduct of similar cases nationwide and, we hope, has thus been of service to libraries and other cultural repositories.

What have we learned and what can we say to others facing similar problems? From our experience, I offer several recommendations that may help both to keep the barn doors closed and to find the pathways most likely to retrieve the livestock should you be unlucky enough to experience a theft.

First, know as much as possible about your collections. Having up-to-date cataloging data is essential. The fact that some of our records for the Arabic material were incomplete or confusing, for example, made it difficult to track that material, some of which has not yet been recovered. In the absence of catalog records, other records are important, such as vertical file folders, publication information, notes from users, and dealer descriptions. Second, keep appraisals of your most valuable materials up to date and readily available, because law enforcement agencies may not be able to pursue cases if the items stolen do not have a predetermined market value. We spent days and days working on valuations, becoming indebted along the way to scores of dealers, auctioneers, and professional appraisers, who, because they were working without seeing the items, were understandably reluctant to give estimates. None of such information about rare items should be kept with the items, nor should it be easily accessible. (We have guessed that in some cases, documents and codices were stolen solely because exhibition labels housed in their boxes identified the materials and explained their importance.)

Next, establish good relations with your institution's legal counsel, security division, risk management office, and administration before a theft occurs. We spent hours explaining what we had, what our procedures were, and how rare books libraries operated to university officials, who, on the one hand, had no idea that such valuable material was present on campus and, on the other hand, did not understand why we had not instantly perceived the loss. Working with the university's office of the general counsel and the public information office would have been much easier had they been primed ahead of time about the use and storage of our collections. The security staff should be familiar with your physical space and aware of any particular areas of vulnerability. It also helps to have a library security officer in place in a time of crisis to deal with law enforcement agencies and attorneys.

Be as open as possible about a theft should one occur, and be prepared to argue for such openness against those who object to reporting an incident for fear that the institution's public name will be tarnished. The practice of keeping things quiet in the hope of avoiding publicity is old-fashioned and counterproductive. Negative consequences are bound to happen when a theft occurs—donor complaints, for example, and alumni headshaking—but they are, on the whole, trivial next to the problems that arise from concealment or evasion. We found the thief and recovered some of the materials only because we published a list of what was lost on the Internet within forty-eight hours of discovery of the loss and followed it up with personal letters to dealers and publication in professional journals. When, however, we agreed to the request of the public information office that a statement to the general interest media, that is, an official press release, not be issued unless newspapers called us (which at first they did not), some faculty members were distressed at not being informed and called a reporter themselves, which led to awkwardness all around. Moreover, we are convinced that the only way to ensure that thefts of cultural material are treated seriously, without silly jokes about overdue library books—as appeared after the Blumberg theft—is to take a strong public stand in defense of library resources.

Our story is not over: there are many unanswered questions. Two months after the April 1998 sentencing, a front-page article in the *New York Times* revealed that one of the lawyers in the case had not really been a lawyer at all and that Spiegelman thus might be entitled to a retrial. Fortunately, this did not happen. Then, in October 1999, I was called by an autograph dealer in Connecticut, Basil Panagopolous, who had been offered some of our unrecovered documents. Spiegelman had escaped from his work release program in Manhattan, had retrieved materials from some secret cache, and had crossed state lines to sell them. He was given a twenty-four-month sentence on May 24, 2000, by Judge Loretta Preska, with three years of probation to follow. Although he claims to have sold everything, we suspect that many things remain in his possession.

Although in retrospect it seems predictable, we have been astonished, ruefully amused, and a bit uncomfortable to observe that the criminal and the crime itself seem to have achieved a life of their own. Diane Johnson's recent novel *Le Mariage* turns on the theft of a medieval manuscript by an American and a subsequent murder.[4] When apprehended, the miscreant is happy to be in the Netherlands because he cannot be extradited to a country where the death penalty might be imposed, a detail clearly derived from newspaper coverage of the Columbia theft. When I discussed the Columbia case with Miles Harvey, the author of a recent book on the Gilbert Bland thefts, he suggested that I do an Internet search for Spiegelman's name.[5] We found a seemingly endless and self-perpetuating list of Web sites suggesting that Spiegelman's involvement in the Oklahoma City bombing was being covered up by the United States government, that his theft was intended to fund that tragic event, and that he was quite possibly the elusive John Doe Number Five. We have downloaded the contents of well over eighty sites for reference, but our file on the case is still open.[6]

10. The Federal Bureau of Investigation's Art Theft Program

 Lynne Chaffinch

On St. Patrick's Day 1990, two men disguised as police officers broke into the Isabella Stewart Gardner Museum in Boston, Massachusetts, and stole twelve pieces of art valued at approximately $300 million. The paintings—including works by Rembrandt, Degas, Manet, and Vermeer—have never been recovered.

The illicit trade in art and cultural property has become a major category of international crime. This includes theft of individual works of art, illegal export of objects protected by international laws, pillaging of archaeological sites, and vandalism. Art crime is an international problem requiring cooperation at all levels of law enforcement. To aid in this endeavor, the Federal Bureau of Investigation (FBI) established the Art Theft Program in 1992 to assist law enforcement agencies investigating these cases. A major component of the Art Theft Program is the National Stolen Art File, a computerized database of stolen art and cultural property as reported to the FBI by law enforcement agencies throughout the United States and internationally. Thefts from museums and libraries account for approximately 18 percent of the cultural property theft cases reported to the National Stolen Art File.

Every institution that maintains collections is at risk from theft. As public awareness increases regarding the institution's responsibility to manage its collections, the institution's staff is under more rigorous requirements to protect the collections. Law enforcement agencies work closely with cultural institutions and rare book and art dealers nationally and internationally to attempt to track down perpetrators of such thefts and to recover stolen cultural property.

To assist cultural institutions in understanding federal laws and reporting procedures concerning theft of cultural property, I shall first describe governing statutes, then give guidelines for responding to an incident of art crime and procedures for reporting the theft to law enforcement officials, and, finally, describe databases regarding stolen art.

The Theft of Major Artwork statute was signed into law in 1994, making it a federal offense to steal from museums and libraries. Following is a summary of the specifics of the statute:

Title 18, United States Code, Section 668—Theft of Major Artwork—makes it a federal offense to obtain by theft or fraud any object of cultural heritage from a museum. The statute also prohibits the "fencing" or possession of such objects, knowing them to be stolen. In defining what constitutes such an institution for its purposes, the statute states that "museum" means an organized and permanent institution, the activities of which affect interstate or foreign commerce, that satisfies the following requirements:

(a) it is situated in the United States;

(b) it is established for an essentially educational or aesthetic purpose;

(c) it has a professional staff; and

(d) it owns, uses, and cares for tangible objects that are exhibited to the public on a regular schedule.

An "object of cultural heritage" means an object that is:

(a) over 100 years old and worth in excess of $5,000; or
(b) worth at least $100,000.

The statute describes two offenses. One results when someone steals or obtains by fraud from the care, custody, or control of a museum any object of cultural heritage. The second involves knowing that an object of cultural heritage has been stolen or obtained by fraud.

Title 18, United States Code, Section 3294, states that no person shall be prosecuted, tried, or punished for a violation of or conspiracy to violate Section 668 unless the indictment is returned or the information is filed within twenty years after the commission of the offense.

Title 18, United States Code, Section 659—Theft from Interstate Shipment—makes it a federal offense to steal or obtain by fraud anything from a conveyance, depot, or terminal, any shipment being transported in interstate or foreign commerce. The statute also prohibits the fencing of such stolen property. Section 1951—Interference with Commerce by Threats of Violence (the Hobbs Act)—makes it a federal offense to obstruct interstate commerce by robbery or extortion or to use or threaten to use violence against any person or property in interstate commerce. Likewise, Sections 2314 and 2315, regarding interstate transportation of stolen property, prohibit the transportation in interstate or foreign commerce of any goods with a value of $5,000 or more by anyone knowing the goods to be stolen. These statutes also prohibit the fencing of such goods.

Illegal Trafficking in Native American Human Remains and Cultural Items, Section 1170, prohibits the sale of the human remains or cultural artifacts of Native Americans without the right of possession of those items in accordance with the Native American Graves Protection and Repatriation Act. Finally, Title 18, United States Code, Sections 641 and 2114—Theft of Government Property—make it illegal to steal or embezzle any government property or to commit robbery of government property.

The FBI has prepared guidelines for responding to the theft of cultural property and for reporting the theft to law enforcement officials. Before a theft occurs, it is important that an institution protect itself by appropriate actions. These are listed here.

(1) Catalog all collections and maintain a backup copy of object records. Include in the physical description: type of object, title, maker, date or period, materials or techniques, measurements, inscriptions and markings, distinguishing features, subject, short description, and image of the object.

(2) Review security procedures for exhibitions, collection storage areas, and transportation of objects. Include registrars or collections managers, curators, security personnel, and administrators in the review process. Administrators should be present so that they are made aware of security concerns and allocate funds to these areas. Update authorization levels and access procedures to collection areas for staff and visitors. Monitor or escort people entering collections storage, including volunteers, researchers, and VIPs. Upgrade access doors to card readers, or change locks at regular intervals, and immediately after a key is lost or an employee is terminated. Document which keys, cards, and access cards are in the possession of each staff member. Evaluate security equipment and repair anything inoperable. Assess exhibition areas to ensure that display cases are secure and objects are protected by barriers, security alarms, or both. Request funding to upgrade security systems as needed. Evaluate security around the outside of the building.

(3) Check employment references and perform criminal history checks on all employees.

(4) Prepare an institutional emergency plan that addresses property theft. Contact local law enforcement agencies and establish liaison with the officers who would respond to matters of cultural property theft at your museum or library. Include their names and contact numbers in the emergency plan, along with the telephone number for the local FBI office. Update contact information every six months. Invite law enforcement officers to visit the museum or library before an incident occurs. Discuss the institution's mission and collections and review possible threats to the collections.

(5) Keep in regular contact with local law enforcement agencies, and stay informed regarding possible threats to the institution. Law enforcement can provide intelligence on gang activity in the area and advise institutions if increases in criminal activity are occurring. They can also inform the institution of local events that may pose a security concern, such as a large parade or festival.

(6) Request your fine arts insurance company to conduct a walk-through of the institution to evaluate the security of the collections. Document any comments for improving security of the collections, and evaluate implementation of suggestions.

(7) Make staff aware of security concerns and request that they contact the appropriate staff member if they see anything suspicious. Create an incident form that can be completed when events occur in the institution.

(8) Perform visual inventory and spot checks of the collections on exhibition and in storage.

When a theft occurs, there are a number of actions the FBI recommends, as follows:

(1) Protect the scene of the crime, and do not let staff or visitors into the area to disturb evidence.

(2) Call the local police department immediately.

(3) Call the local FBI office if the stolen objects fulfill the criteria under the Theft of Major Artwork provision (Title 18, United States Code, Section 668). The object must be more than 100 years old and valued in excess of $5,000 or worth at least $100,000. For thefts outside the United States, the FBI maintains more than thirty legal attaché offices overseas, which can process requests for assistance with cultural property thefts.

(4) Determine the last time the objects were seen and what happened in the area, or to the objects, since that time.

(5) Identify witnesses and gather all pertinent information regarding the theft and suspect or suspects for the law enforcement agency.

(6) Prepare written descriptions of stolen objects for the police, including photographs of objects if available.

(7) Contact the donors or lenders, if applicable, to advise them of the theft.

(8) Contact the insurance company and file an insurance claim.

(9) Complete an incident report for internal use.

As regards recovery from a theft, the FBI recommends that a museum:

(1) Evaluate the theft and determine continuing threats to the collections. Update security policies or equipment, if necessary.

(2) Prepare statements for the media, and plan the institution's strategy for dealing with public relations issues.

(3) Prepare a theft report having images and descriptions of stolen objects and distribute the report to museums, libraries, auction houses, dealers, galleries, and collectors who may be offered the objects for sale. Coordinate with the investigating agency.

(4) Perform follow-up with the law enforcement agency,

and request updated reports on the progress of the investigation.

An important resource is the National Stolen Art File (NSAF). This database was developed as a law enforcement tool. Therefore, only law enforcement agencies can submit requests to add objects to the database or to have the database searched. The file lists case information, including suspects and modus operandi, and provides object descriptions and images. Victims of theft should check with the investigating officer to make sure that the officer is aware of the database and that information about stolen objects is submitted to the FBI Art Theft Program by the investigating officer. The FBI also maintains a Web page with art theft notices listed at <www.fbi.gov>. Institutions can request that their objects be placed on the notices that are distributed through the investigating agency.

The file is located in Washington, D.C., at the address National Stolen Art File, Federal Bureau of Investigation, Major Theft Unit, room 5096, 935 Pennsylvania Avenue, NW, Washington, D.C. 20535. The telephone number is (202) 324-4192, and the fax number is (202) 324-1504. Additional information regarding the NSAF can be found on the FBI Web page, <www.fbi.gov>, under the heading "Headquarters and Programs/Criminal Investigative Division."

The Art Loss Register (ALR) is a private company funded primarily by insurance companies. The ALR conducts searches of its database for auction houses, museums conducting due diligence searches during provenance research and acquisitions, and private individuals. Further information can be found at the ARL Web site, <www.artloss.com>. The address is Art Loss Register, 20 East Forty-sixth Street, suite 1402, New York, N.Y. 10017. The telephone number is (212) 297-0941, and the fax number is (212) 972-5091.

The Interpol Cultural Property Database is a database

maintained by Interpol Headquarters, Lyon, France, with access through Interpol Washington, D.C. Requests for objects to be added to the database or searches to be performed must be made through a law enforcement agency. Objects listed on this database are those that may be shipped overseas for possible sale. The address is Interpol Washington, U.S. National Central Bureau, 1301 New York Avenue, Fourth floor, Washington, D.C. 20530. The telephone numbers are (202) 616-9000 and, for faxes, (202) 616-8400.

In addition, there are other smaller, specialized databases for stolen art, where an institution may want to register its stolen objects. Staff supporting the databases listed above may be able to assist theft victims in identifying the appropriate databases to contact.

11. The Silver Lining

Recovering from the Shambles of a Disaster

 Camila A. Alire

No one immediately involved in a major crisis or disaster even begins to think about whether or not the crisis might have some silver lining. That is the last thing on anyone's mind.

This was definitely the case at Morgan Library at Colorado State University in July 1997, when half its collections were damaged by flood waters. Staff members found themselves overwhelmed in emergency disaster recovery, in designing innovative systems to recover damaged materials, and in creating emergency programs to serve library users during the disaster recovery period. Be assured that there was no silver lining at the outset.

From this experience, however, the Morgan Library was able to take a major disaster and turn the experience into something positive. Staff members were able to convert the cards dealt them into positive strategies and results and share their experience with other institutions as a model response to a major disaster.

The crisis began on the evening of July 27, 1997, when Fort Collins, Colorado, suffered flash flooding and, in a period of four hours, received 6.5 inches of rain. The Morgan Library was hit hard:

> At about 10:30 [P.M.], the pressure of tons of water caused a portion of the west wall of the lower level [of Morgan Library] to give way, allowing the water to cascade in. Unlike a normal flood, where water slowly rises, a flash flood raged through the lower level. Later, estimates by the city indicated that the water entered the building at 5,000 cubic feet per minute—flood stage on the local Cache La Poudre River is measured at 3,000 cubic feet per minute.[1]

The water level within the Library's lower level rose 8.5 feet, rising above the ceiling tiles by six inches. Some 658 cubic feet of water were in the library, equaling 4.9 million gallons, or 41 million pounds. All the bound journals housed in the library were damaged and had to be removed from the building, as were all the monographs located on the lower level. Afterward, many subject disciplines had no materials available for researchers.

Even though the disaster struck three weeks before the fall semester, the university president mandated that all buildings damaged must be operational by the first day of classes. Morgan Library was the hardest hit building on campus.

Although there have been larger-scale library disasters than that at Morgan Library, no one had ever attempted to recover and restore close to 500,000 water-damaged volumes and return them to the collection. Ours was a pioneering effort, and because of that, there were no libraries we could consult about engaging in this monumental project.

In the crisis, public relations efforts were focused on three levels: information to staff affected; information to the parent organization; and information to the external community. Morgan Library staff worked hard to ensure that there was no negative press about the library's disaster that could affect enrollment of students for the academic year. Communication of information to all interested parties was forthcoming and provided the key to developing strong relationships with campus administrators, campus community, library users, and the public press.

The university faculty should be a key focus for media relations for any research library that suffers extensive damage to its collection. The communication relationship the library develops with its teaching and research faculty is critical. A silver lining here was the existence of the University Faculty Council's Committee on Libraries and the role it developed in cooperation with library administrators to keep faculty and students informed about disaster recovery efforts and progress.

"All potential spokespersons . . . should be media trained in advance."[2] We had our silver lining in this case in place before the disaster occurred. That is, the library dean had received basic media training through the American Library Association's advocacy training program. This training was critical in establishing the credibility of a new library dean with her staff, the university administration, university faculty, the press, and the external community. The university's office of media relations relied on the library dean to speak for the university concerning the recovery at Morgan Library.

Can our discovery of this silver lining, based on the Morgan Library experience, help other libraries in the future? Yes. All organizations dealing with the stewardship of cultural resources that could experience possible crises related to those resources should have key personnel who are media-trained. In addition, a basic media relations plan should be developed to handle potential disasters or crises.[3]

Chaos existed during the immediate emergency disaster recovery period, which lasted for the three weeks before the fall semester began. Morgan Library staff members immediately began working on restoring public services. That was the first priority, and there was no doubt that library services tied to the opening of the facility would be restored. The major issue for public service, however, was how to meet the research and curricular needs of the students and faculty when one-half of the Library's collections were gone.

Colorado State University is a Research I institution with Association of Research Libraries (ARL) membership, and the disaster brought a huge demand for interlibrary loans (ILL). Even though Morgan Library was lucky to have an innovative, progressive, and almost totally automated interlibrary loan department, it had to change its procedures during the emergency, and from this emerged a facet of the silver lining.

First, the library completely overhauled ILL processing routines to maximize efficiency by automating all phases of the process that allowed long-term applications. Not only were new automation and programming efforts developed specifically for disaster recovery ILL services, but the changes were also intentionally designed to introduce permanent improvement in ILL service.[4]

Second, the library's ILL disaster recovery services involved the new FastFlood document delivery service. This totally automated service delivered journal articles in two days or less 95 percent of the time to Colorado State University (CSU) users. Its efficiency has raised the expectations of our users for desktop article delivery. Both CSU students and faculty members have displayed such enthusiastic appreciation for this streamlined service that the FastFlood model is being integrated into our ILL service over the long term. The university has provided funding for Morgan Library to work with six other ARL libraries to develop our system into a national delivery model entitled Project RAPID.

Third, Morgan Library's public service culture became suffused with a new emphasis on the convenience of the user. Since the disaster, the public service staff has become increasingly enthusiastic about implementing new services. Staff members demonstrate far greater willingness to take risks. They avoid overburdening new programs with rules and regulations. Staff members deliberately devise more user-friendly policies and procedures for users.

Because most of the disaster recovery projects have affected the technical services division of Morgan Library and because that is where the library's disaster planning and recovery leaders are employed, much of the stress has been experienced in this area. Even in technical services, however, a silver lining has revealed itself.

The system design of various phases of massive recovery and restoration of water-damaged materials could serve as a model. Design techniques created for the recovery contractor and his staff for implementation were based on preservation principles.

Technical services staff members were ingenious in developing concepts that helped cover recovery costs. They used a "value loss" concept, applying it to each damaged volume, which was critical in negotiations with the insurance carrier.

Additionally, the staff introduced the "fat factor" concept. The fat factor is the actual swelling factor that wet books experience after they are dry. A sampling of damaged books compared with undamaged books of the exact title demonstrated a 16 percent average fat factor, which was then converted into expanded space requirements. We used a formula to support our additional needs, and university negotiators were successful in convincing the insurance carrier of the need to cover costs for additional space at the library's off-site depository.

Another aspect of the silver lining in technical services relates to collaboration with commercial library vendors. The technical services staff's use of automation to output files for comparisons to these vendors has given the library an opportunity to look differently at vendor relationships in the future.

Using this information, the staff was able to assess and approach various vendors for potentially responding with a proposal for involvement in the last phase of recovery.

In any disaster, the type of insurance coverage is critical, and valuing a library's collection is much more difficult than assessing value for a physical facility. Morgan Library's insurance coverage for its collection was better than most libraries. The university's risk management and inventory values covered a set value per volume as well as including a "back-to-original-condition" clause. This clause alone prompted library officials to urge university negotiators to negotiate for a value loss figure of $6 million.

The library staff's involvement was critical in the development of cost studies with a statistics consultant. Staff collaboration included preparing cost models for university negotiators to negotiate with the insurance carrier. The silver lining in this case was the reexamination of ways in which the library's physical collection should be valued for the future. Consequently, the library developed better estimates of the collections costs than ever before.[5]

A related benefit that may profit other libraries was derived from these studies about determining the value of a library's collection. It is critical to recognize the importance of insuring a library collection at its proper value and developing an insurance policy that covers the true costs of collection loss.

In the first few weeks of disaster recovery, library disaster consultants from all over the country adamantly insisted that the total loss percentage of the collection damaged would be around 10 to 20 percent. Morgan Library administrators disagreed, predicting anywhere from 30 to 40 percent total losses. The university administration and insurance representatives accepted the consultants' figures. Morgan Library's total loss is now teetering around 35 percent to date. When one thinks about a total loss of materials edging on 40 percent, it would seem difficult to find any semblance of a silver lining.

With total loss at such a large percentage, we needed to look at reshaping Morgan Library's research collection, heading toward new directions for collection building. Therein lies our silver lining. Morgan Library selectors are focusing on two areas for reshaping the collection for the future. One focus is to rethink the material type—choosing, perhaps, more electronic alternatives, which may tip the balance between electronic resources and print material. The other focus is to look at the future of CSU's curricular and research needs in reshaping the overall collection.

In terms of electronic resources, Morgan Library received special, subsidized access to a variety of electronic databases and full-text resources. In this way, Morgan Library staff members and users had an opportunity to experiment with a wide array of electronic options and, in the process, expanded their willingness to give serious consideration to electronic alternatives. And yet, this expanded knowledge pointed also to the value of traditional materials. "Conversely, the most radical electronic champions, among both staff and users, have had their expectations tempered by a new perceived reality—even when the opportunity presented itself, it was seen that electronic resources could not come close to substituting for a research collection built over decades of planned acquisitions."[6]

The biggest factor in the silver lining found in restoring Morgan Library's collection involved the response to the library's aggressive gift-solicitation project. This project resulted in replacing 100,000 exact-title, undamaged volumes for damaged serials and monographs by substitute volumes. The country—libraries, professors, professional societies, commercial publishers, and so forth—responded overwhelmingly to the library's request for donation of exact-title gift materials. Not only did donors send exact titles, but they also donated other titles as well. Such a donor response to the Library's disaster had an additional silver lining. It was a much-needed morale booster for library administrators, faculty, and staff.

One can only imagine the despair experienced by an entire library staff when the extent of such library damage is shared with them. There are no words to capture the overwhelming feelings and fears everyone experiences. However, here too there was a silver lining.

First, not only did the library's disaster recovery team have a disaster plan and recovery document, but it also had gone through disaster recovery practice drills. Even more important, several members of the team had served as presenters at disaster-planning workshops earlier in the year. Morgan Library staff was as well prepared for a disaster as any group could be.

Library staff members worked increasingly in teams to solve problems and sharpened their negotiation and planning skills. Cross-training was introduced immediately after the disaster and is now standard practice in the organization. Overall, the silver lining for personnel is summarized by the comment that "Little stuff doesn't faze us! Throughout the Library, staff at all levels were called on to do things—different thinking, reports, analyses, projects—that they normally wouldn't do. Professional and leadership skills of many staff were challenged and improved. Staff have grown in confidence about their abilities."[7]

Second, the disaster changed the culture of the organization of the library. Many staff members were involved in developing a more innovative approach to problem solving.[8] Staff members devised and implemented systems for projects that had never been considered before in major library disaster recovery. Most important, staff members became more adaptable and flexible, more open to change.

Two related special projects evolved from the disaster. The

first project is called GAP—the gift augmentation project. As mentioned previously, the donor response to the Library's gift solicitation project netted many more new-title volumes. Because of that, the university administration became amenable to funding GAP, which involves first selecting titles that will enhance the overall collection and then processing them into the library's collection.

The second project is one that we hope will help other libraries. The monograph entitled *Library Disaster Planning and Recovery Handbook* was developed and written by members of the library's disaster recovery team in 1998 so that they could share their experiences with others. The book has already had an effect on other disaster recovery efforts. North Dakota State University's library suffered flood damage in the summer of 2000, and its library administrators used the handbook to assist them in their recovery efforts.

And so, from that day in July 1997 when its collections were so badly damaged, Morgan Library took a major disaster and found the silver lining that resulted from disaster recovery. In rebuilding its collections to developing new systems, in changing the institutional culture to bring greater collaboration and flexibility, in developing a handbook so that others could benefit from the library's experience—Morgan Library found the silver lining that grew out of what at first seemed a disaster of overwhelming proportions.

BUILDING THE BUDGET

*Promoting Your Program and Meeting Funding
Demands for Preservation and Security*

12. Funding for Preservation

The Strengths of Our Past

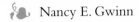 Nancy E. Gwinn

Cultural institutions of all kinds—whether libraries, archives, museums, or organizations interested in preserving historic houses—take seriously their roles as preservers and protectors of our cultural heritage. Those of us who work professionally in these organizations find ourselves coping with an innate conflict: the desire to protect at odds with the desire to share with others what we are protecting.

This was brought home to me recently when I read a wonderful novel by a young writer, Elizabeth McCracken, whose narrator and protagonist Peggy Cort is a public librarian. What Peggy Cort muses about rings true, at least to this librarian, especially when she says, "There is nothing I can't make into a library in my brain, no objects I don't imagine borrowing or lending out. Not out of generosity—I am a librarian, and protective—but out of a sense of strange, careful justice. Part of me believes that all material things belong to all people."[1]

Although my own experience is definitely library based, since 1984 I have practiced my profession in the middle of the largest museum complex in the world: the Smithsonian Institution. My discussion is based on this experience.

First, let us take a brief look at the past. In the early nineteenth century, about fifty years after Independence Day and after we had repelled the several attempts of the British and French to reverse our course, intellectual leaders in the United States began to promote and build our own American cultural institutions, mirroring those of Europe. First, Benjamin Franklin worked toward establishing scientific and learned societies like Philadelphia's American Philosophical Society and the Academy of Natural Sciences. Then, libraries grew to useful size at places like Harvard and Yale, the Smithsonian Institution, the Library of Congress, the New York State Library, and the public libraries of New York and Boston. Along with these, developed museums of natural history and art.

An assumption about all of these institutions was that they would be places of intellectual ferment stimulated by their making available works or collections of the past, which they had a mission to protect and keep secure for the purpose of continuing enlightenment. Notice that I do not say "preserve" or "conserve," because these are words that have come to the fore mainly in the twentieth century, after scientific investigation began to expose the fact that simply securing these collections was insufficient to ensure their longevity. Indeed, collections were vulnerable to many problems, either inherent or caused by the actions of the past.

In the 1960s, William Barrow published results of tests of aging and strength of paper that indisputably revealed the problems of high acid content in nineteenth-century books. Similarly, early naturalists, who wanted to preserve animal skins collected by the U.S. Exploring Expedition of the 1840s, ordered for the purpose "whiskey, a corrosive sublimate, and arsenic."[2] Early filmmakers used highly flammable nitrate films. Builders proudly poured asbestos into buildings to protect them from fire. What used to be a matter of storage and security has become a preservation problem, and an expensive one, for us today, not only because of the techniques required but because collections have a way of growing, and growing, and growing, even as they age, and age, and age.

What is a library or museum to do these days, particularly as we are not in an era that values preservation in and of itself, but only when connected with use? Libraries and museums are facing incredible pressures to make their collections—or perhaps I should say "content"—easily available. They must find a way to remain important, credible institutions in a digital world. They must compete successfully with the many new distractions of our modern age. All of this requires money. All of this strains budgets that may not be receiving the same level of support from traditional government sources or fund-raising mechanisms. If costs are going up and budgets are flat, it is difficult to argue the need for preservation support or to prevent budget cuts. Collections may be grouped, along with buildings, as targets for deferred maintenance. Can we wait one more year before getting the roof fixed? Can we wait one more year before deacidifying those manuscripts? As a manager faced with difficult choices, I might well look at things this way. But as someone dedicated to preservation, instead I look for opportunities. And in today's environment, I think there are many.

In 2000, the Association of Research Libraries (ARL) surveyed its members to study their perceptions regarding the status of preservation programs. The eighty-seven members who responded pointed to a relatively upbeat picture, indicating some real achievements over the preceding five years. Sixty of the members reported significant or moderate change, and much of it was quite positive. For example:

- Nine libraries reported establishment of new preservation departments or programs, having created eight new jobs for preservation librarians. Only one program had been eliminated.

- Twenty-nine libraries reported either that their preservation budgets had grown or that funding had stabilized, and four libraries reported that they had received preservation endowments.

- Twenty-four institutions had added a digitizing capacity to their preservation programs.

- Twenty-two had built new or expanded facilities, usually conservation laboratories, and another fourteen had improved their environments with air-conditioning or new storage facilities.

- Twenty institutions had increased microfilming production or quality.

Did their preservation programs meet their needs, the ARL members were asked? "Yes," said thirty respondents. "No" said another thirty, and twenty-two said, "Yes, but only in some areas." Nearly half the ARL members think they have a way to go before they feel that the appropriate balance of preservation and other programs will be met.

Where did they see their challenges? It is not surprising that lack of funding came at the top of the list, followed by the issue of how to preserve and archive digital materials—something that would not have even occurred as an issue a decade ago. And lest we feel we have taken care of the traditional problems, twenty-six members reported that the number of brittle books in their collections was growing. Others reported poor environmental controls because of aging facilities and problems with heating, venting, and air-conditioning (HVAC) systems; the difficulty of hiring and retaining quality staff; and obstacles to preserving non-book formats such as videos and sound recordings.

What will be the greatest influence on the future of preservation programs? Again, the members pointed to funding as most important, along with the growth of digital technologies, followed closely by management vision and staffing levels.

There have been gains, but these results clearly show that we must not rest on our laurels. Much of our success has grown out of infusions of funding in the 1980s from external sources, notably the National Endowment for the Humanities (NEH), the Andrew W. Mellon Foundation, and the U.S. Department of Education. Funding is still available from those sources. Living in the midst of a museum community, however, without access to federal sources for grant funds such as these, and largely unable to tap into local community foundations given our federal status, I have begun to look much harder for other sources of funds—in particular to the individual donor. I suspect that the preservation endowments that are beginning to appear, and to which I referred earlier, are coming from private sources.

An example of how investment in preservation can pay off not only in the work on collections but as a fund-raising tool is found in my own experience. When I arrived at the Smithsonian in 1984, I was fresh from several years at the Research Libraries Group, focusing on helping institutions establish and fund microfilming programs. I discovered that the Smithsonian Libraries had two preservation units: a commercial binding section and a book conservation laboratory. Although the Smithsonian is a very large institution with more than six thousand employees, the Smithsonian Libraries is a smaller unit, with about 120 staff members, a budget today approaching just $8 million, about 80 percent of which goes into personnel, and a collection of just over 1.5 million volumes. Despite a substantial special collections department, it seemed quite a luxury for an institution our size to have a book conservation laboratory. In an environment surrounded by museums that put a premium on artifact conservation, and where there were a number of other conservation laboratories, having our own was questionable. I focused my attention first on the general collections and on its preservation problems, hoping to enlarge the preservation program.

I used a standard approach. With the help of ARL, the Smithsonian Libraries undertook a year-long preservation planning program, during which we gathered considerable data about our collections and in particular about the large percentage of books that were brittle. We were prepared to catch the wave of congressional interest in brittle books as a national problem. Unfortunately, we were not eligible for the funds that Congress began to appropriate to NEH in the early 1980s to fund the initiative. We were ready, however, when, in our congressional appropriations hearing, the committee chairman suddenly asked out of the blue if the Smithsonian had any brittle books. Within months, we had received appropriated funds to start a brittle-books program.

Even with those funds, the amount of material we could preserve was small, compared with the need. So we looked for other sources and focused on collections unique to the Smithsonian and on preservation proposals that could be packaged and marketed to have a broad appeal. One such was our world's fair collections, about twenty-five hundred items dating from the Crystal Palace Exhibition in London in 1851 through the Panama-Pacific Exhibition in San Francisco in 1915. This proved attractive to a commercial microfilming company, which microfilmed the collection and marketed it as "The Books of the Fairs." The microfilm sold well, and we received royalties. This publication project stimulated a variety of other activities, including publication of two books, an exhibition, and a symposium.

This saved me from having to siphon funds from the book conservation laboratory for what at the time I perceived to be a much greater need. And thank goodness for that. The laboratory has always done superb work. It was not until I began to actively raise funds for it, however, that I truly understood its appeal in this regard.

In short, potential donors love the lab. When the book

conservation laboratory is listed as one of the options on a Smithsonian Behind-the-Scenes tour, it is always oversubscribed. Most people have no understanding of how books are constructed or how you can preserve them by taking them apart, washing and cleaning the paper, filling in holes, sewing—think of that, sewing—them back together, and creating a new binding. I found it much easier to sell the concept of preservation as a whole when we returned to the idea of the book as artifact. Having a conservator on board to show these techniques made clear more than anything else the commitment and seriousness of purpose a library has toward preservation.

The laboratory as a wonderful tour and demonstration site is only one of its values. Remember that when an annual budget is being apportioned, the first thing to be covered is personnel. When I queried several of my museum colleagues as I prepared this paper about how they budgeted for preservation, they said they did not. First, they covered the staff payroll, then they looked at what was needed for upcoming exhibitions in the museum. They had conservators on staff, and what was conserved, or stabilized, was driven by the exhibition needs, including items to be lent for exhibition elsewhere. My colleagues did not look at it as budgeting for preservation. They looked at it as a normal part of their operation.

The Smithsonian Libraries began a serious exhibition program around 1990, using a small gallery in the National Museum of American History, now known also as the Kenneth J. Behring Center. I found that exhibition needs became a driver for our program as well, at least for the book conservation laboratory. In fact, I doubt if we could maintain a gallery without our own conservators, not only to restore, stabilize, or safeguard the items to be displayed, but also to create mounts, monitor light levels, and reduce risk as much as possible. But that has its benefits, because the exhibition gallery gives us visibility, creates opportunities for entertaining prospective donors, and helps raise the awareness of senior administrators and other staff to what we have in our collections. To mount a good exhibition requires funding, and when you raise money for an exhibition, you can build in a budget for conservation.

What are the lessons to be drawn from this experience? It may not be what you think, because I understand that not all libraries have the collections that require the skills of professional book conservators. First, you need to have the facts about your collection, so an investment into learning those facts, as we did with our planning program, can prepare you for walking through the door of an opportunity that is unexpected. Second, whether you are trying to convince senior managers of the importance of allocating funds to preservation, whether as a manager you are trying to defend a preservation budget, or whether you are trying to convince a donor of the worthiness of a preservation endowment, there is a powerful emotional appeal attached to the artifact, to the traditional role of libraries in preserving books and in demonstrating to a public how that is done. Museums understand the power of the original; libraries can use it as well.

At least for a couple of generations, I think we will see more and more interest in books and book preservation. If you present and package the need to donors carefully, they will understand the value of preservation endowments that can then be used to cover multiple preservation needs, including microfilming, digitizing, environmental monitoring, and book restoration. Maybe in our scramble toward a digital future, we should think about, capitalize on, and market for new audiences the strengths of our past.

13. **Securing Preservation Funds** · *National and Institutional Requirements*

 Deanna B. Marcum

Focusing on a national rather than an institutional perspective toward the subject of funding for the work of preservation is an opportunity I welcome. Such funding is a major concern for me personally and for the organization I represent, the Council on Library and Information Resources (CLIR), a private nonprofit organization that gets people together to work on issues affecting the ability of libraries and archives to serve their constituencies. Preservation funding is certainly such an issue, and we have long been involved. The council came into being through the recombination of the Council on Library Resources and the Commission on Preservation and Access, which the council earlier had organized to concentrate on such problems as how to prevent the loss of massive collections printed on acidic paper. The CLIR as a whole continues to promote attention to "brittle books," along with many other preservation concerns, including the problems of preserving increasing quantities of digitized information.

Is funding adequate for dealing with such needs? Far from it. Not that there is active opposition. Nearly everyone regards preservation as a good thing. Who is not in favor of preserving the intellectual and cultural record, the materials on which teaching and research depend, the heritage of centuries of civilization? The fact that it is considered a good thing has not, however, been sufficient to guarantee adequate funding for preservation in American research institutions.

Preservation funding is, in fact, imperiled. Throughout the 1980s and into the 1990s, the majority of major research libraries in the United States developed preservation programs. Advocacy for meeting preservation needs came from several national organizations along with mine, and providers of funds both in the private sector and in government responded with support. The National Endowment for the Humanities, to take a prominent example, began in 1988 its program of grant-making for microfilming deteriorating books and newspaper collections.

But support peaked early in the 1990s and now seems in relative decline. A report issued in 1999 on preserving research collections found that preservation expenditures in member institutions of the Association of Research Libraries (ARL) have been little more than level since 1993, despite growth in total materials expenditures. The report also found that external funding for preservation has declined steadily and that staffing has declined as well.[1] The most recently published ARL preservation statistics show a significant decrease also in the volume of microfilming activity.[2]

Why these discouraging developments? Preservation funding is imperiled for a number of reasons. First, private funding tends to follow trends, and currently there is keen interest in digitization as a means of making materials accessible to new and broader audiences. Consequently, access projects are far more likely than preservation projects to succeed in the competitive review process. Although the Andrew W. Mellon Foundation, for example, continues to be supportive of preservation work, funding for microfilming has been redirected to digitization projects.

Second, something similar is happening in federal agencies. The National Endowment for the Humanities (NEH), the Library of Congress, and the Smithsonian Institution have adopted strategies that emphasize access for the K–12 audience as well as for the general public. Such an emphasis on accountability and service to all constituents gives preference to funding requests that enhance access. The strategies to improve access have increased the visibility of these agencies and have led to better relationships with Congress. We can hope that this will eventually lead to greater funding that can be applied also to such important activities as preservation.

Moreover, the stagnation of the NEH budget in recent years has hurt research libraries, which had taken considerable advantage of the Endowment's microfilming support.[3] The NEH preservation microfilming program is within its Division of Preservation and Access. The division's annual allocation within the NEH budget dropped from $22 million in fiscal 1995 to less than $17 million in fiscal 1996, and it rose only slightly above $18 million in the succeeding four fiscal years.[4] Projects to develop tools and resources for scholarship now compete with microfilming for funds available from NEH. And the Institute of Museum and Library Services, which has a funding category for "preservation and digitization," seems thus far to be funding digitization projects only.

Finally, preservation funding suffers because we have not advanced a compelling national plan for preserving important resources. In the absence of such a plan, we are without strategies in which we can collaborate to strengthen our appeal for funding. Projects continue to come piecemeal to funders, unsupported by a context of national urgency, and unrelated to a set of priorities for meeting our massive preservation needs. Overcoming this disability is critical, I believe, for countering the declines I have described in funding—both public and private.

How do we begin such a plan? The Council on Library and Information Resources proposes to collaborate with the Association of Research Libraries, the Oberlin Group of liberal arts colleges, and a group of comprehensive university libraries not members of ARL in a study that will be the first step. Using techniques both quantitative and qualitative, we plan to evaluate current preservation conditions and challenges, identify indicators of health, and recommend means for revitalizing preservation programs. Specific investigations we propose to make include the following:

(1) We must analyze preservation statistics in relation to significant trends affecting American libraries. When in 2000 ARL member libraries reported a decline of 12.5 percent in circulation since 1995 and a significant decline also in purchased volumes (26 percent in monographs and 6 percent in serial titles) since 1986, we had to ask whether there was a concomitant drop in the need for physical preservation.[5] Did these figures correlate with such core preservation activities as binding, pre-shelf processing, and book repair? What effect have major retrospective cataloging projects had on preservation activities, and are these projects nearing completion?

(2) Libraries of all types report significant increases in their digital acquisitions and conversions, but few have developed adequate strategies for digital preservation.[6] What role should preservation programs have in shaping institutional policies for digital preservation? Has there been a shift in preservation resources to meet these needs?

(3) In 1991, ARL issued benchmarks for selected core activities in preservation programs.[7] Are these still valid despite changing circumstances of ownership and access?

(4) We must address the brittle-books strategy developed in the 1980s in light of changing fortunes in NEH and conse-

quent repercussions for funding. Is the strategy compatible with new directions in library preservation programs?

(5) We must ask why institutions are finding it difficult to attract top professionals to preservation positions. What is the state of preservation education in library and information studies programs? What can national professional organizations do to develop preservation leadership skills and revitalize preservation leadership?

(6) Consortial structures for preservation work, such as regional conservation centers, depend heavily on outside funding. The Mellon Foundation is investigating possible business models for greater self-sufficiency. What can we learn from such studies to strengthen cooperative preservation activities? We should study strategies for financing preservation programs that have succeeded in research libraries and how they can be applied elsewhere. Are institutions using local resources for preservation, or do they rely on foundations and other external funds?

Once we have the proposed report's answers to these questions, we will convene a conference of senior preservation administrators, library directors, professional organization representatives, and relevant others. We will ask them to consider, in light of the report's findings, the role and the effectiveness of preservation programs in the digital age. We will challenge them to develop a plan of action for meeting preservation needs in American libraries, archives, and related repositories.

The time for this is now. Even as funding is slipping, digital technologies present new options for efficiency and effectiveness in preservation as well as new technical and conceptual challenges. For example, once a book is digitized and, with proper maintenance, made electronically available indefinitely, will a need remain for every library with a paper copy to invest scant resources in preserving it? Or, would library funds go further if we collectively created national repositories to preserve "artifact" copies of low-use materials, while making electronic or microfilmed copies available to all our patrons?

After all, we are not preserving collections just for the benefit of each of our institutions. We are collectively caring for—and preparing to pass on—the cultural inheritance of our society. We must therefore articulate the urgent need for preservation until it becomes a national priority. Do not conclude that you may safely leave all this to national organizations such as the Council on Library Resources or the Association of Research Libraries. Ultimately, each individual institution must view itself as a contributor to the national collection of accessible scholarly resources, accept responsibility for preserving a share of such materials, collaborate to reduce the burdens of that responsibility, and help make the case for support of this work to those who control resources.

Neither individually nor collectively can we discard our obligations to be stewards of our collections. Preservation continues to be a critically important issue, and we must all accept the responsibility of keeping it in the forefront of our concerns. Funders will find the case for meeting any institution's individual needs more attractive if the contribution you are making to the nation's heritage is justified in terms of collaborative efforts to achieve economies. Together, we can preserve our cultural inheritance.

14. Strategies for Funding Preservation and Security

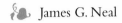 James G. Neal

Library preservation and security programs increasingly compete for resources to meet an expanding array of rigorous collection, service, and technology needs. In a survey of Association of Research Libraries members concerning the future of special collections, lack of funding for preservation was overwhelmingly identified as the leading preservation challenge.[1] Libraries are developing innovative strategies to build budget support and to attract new external funds through grants, statewide initiatives, fund-raising campaigns, and entrepreneurial activities.

As institutional budgets and national funding programs have fallen woefully short of library preservation and security needs, new demands, such as the archiving of digital resources, have only further eroded library capabilities. Few libraries have been able to make a strong case for stewardship of the collection as an integral component of development priorities. Progress will require fiscal agility, innovative packaging of collection and preservation needs, and development of new markets for preservation services.

In this paper, I will outline the range of preservation and

security strategies now available to libraries, the infrastructure and tools needed to advance a successful program, the various audiences requiring education and advocacy, and the core qualities and tensions integral to a library preservation and security effort. I will discuss the way each of these elements intersects with resource development and will describe activities that may be implemented to attract support.

Besides documenting lack of funding as the primary concern, the Association of Research Libraries survey on preservation programs highlighted several additional areas as priority challenges. These include: the preservation and archiving of digital resources, the reformatting of brittle books, the creation and maintenance of appropriate environmental controls, and the recruitment and retention of expert staffing. Each of these broad areas of concern presents not only extraordinary funding needs but also rich opportunities for creative financing.

A preservation program must be presented as a comprehensive strategy, particularly in a research library setting, and all of its core elements must be clearly identified. These elements include, first of all, a collection condition survey and documentation of need. Preventive and stabilization procedures, repair and conservation procedures, reformatting techniques, and environmental monitoring activities are also important. The strategy must embrace as well facility improvements, collection management and handling, and staff training. User education, digital archiving, and disaster preparedness must also be addressed. Each of these many components requires a firm financial commitment.

Preservation strategies should be advanced in the context of a program plan that includes a well-articulated vision and clear priorities for action. The plan must spell out measurable objectives, with supporting documentation and requirements for requisite expertise and essential resources. It should articulate clear and reasonable expectations and include a commitment to assessment. Such a plan can be used to rally institutional support and attract external interest and funding. The essential resources are significant: professional staff, clerical and student staff, equipment, supplies, technology, and facilities are all possible resources.

As the preservation program is built, many important issues must be considered that are linked to resource development. Will the program be comprehensive, or will it specialize in selected areas or activities? Will it focus on the working and circulating collections, or on the special and rare collections? Will the emphasis be on traditional techniques, or on new and experimental strategies? Will the priority be conservation of the original works, or creation of surrogate copies? Will the program champion local needs for preservation, or serve as a model for national programs?

A balance between access to collections and the security of collections must be achieved. Will base budget support be provided, or will the program rely primarily on "soft" and external sources of funds? Will the preservation work be handled by in-house staff, or will operations be outsourced to external individuals and firms? The preservation program might be advanced primarily as an institutional initiative, or consortium approaches might be sought. Will a preservation program be developed, or will preservation activities be carried out as a series of funded projects with one-time financing? Obviously, these questions present choices, and most institutional preservation efforts will prove to be a cross between several options. The orientation of a program must be clearly spelled out, however, because it will drive funding and fundraising decisions.

Less clear are ways to attract external funds to support collection security needs. It may be argued that grants organizations and individual donors view such operations as the core responsibility of the institution. Policies and procedures that manage collection theft, collection mutilation, control of users, control of access, user surveillance, special storage, and the use of surrogate copies might be difficult to sell outside the library. Another new area of concern is the security of electronic data. In all cases, the cost of managing security and the impact of collection loss and damage must be clearly presented.

Grant funding for preservation programs in libraries has traditionally come from several sources, namely, national foundations, family foundations, federal agencies, state legislative projects, or corporations. In general, the interest of these granting agencies has gone from support for institutional preservation programs to national demonstration and leadership projects. The focus is on the clarity of objectives and the project plan, the national contribution and impact of the work, and the significance of the collection being preserved. The innovative application of new technologies, the choice of appropriate strategies, and the availability of necessary resources and expertise are also important to funders. It is important for the institution to establish a record of institutional commitment and accomplishment, appropriate and effective partnerships, and rigorous assessment strategies.

External fund-raising for preservation programs in libraries has also traditionally come from several sources. The support of library friends groups, annual gifts programs, and special project funding are three of these. Others include the creation of preservation endowments for positions or programs, the creation of collection endowments that include preservation components, adopt-a-book programs, planned giving and bequests, and naming opportunities. Libraries that have been successful in attracting support from donors have been able to link collection development and preservation activities, to demonstrate that the purchase of an item for the collection may involve an ongoing responsibility for its maintenance. Libraries also have been able to tap into donor interest in new technologies and the ability to extend and enhance use through digitization while also enabling the preservation of the original artifact.

Library fund-raising for preservation should focus on traditional support groups, those individuals having a strong interest in the book, and "new generation" support, from those individuals who look to the library for leadership in the use of information technology. An important consideration in such fund-raising is the recruitment of unrestricted support that can be used for changing needs and opportunities versus funds that are earmarked for a specific activity or class of materials. In all cases, preservation must be linked to the academic excellence of the institution, to the national significance and impact of the preservation activity, or to the institutional reputation and visibility. Depending on the audience, links to innovation or to historical roles and values are also important.

A new area of external resource development that libraries should advance is entrepreneurial or new market development. Individual libraries may be able to organize preservation services that would be of interest to other libraries, individuals, or organizations. Leveraging assets such as expertise, experience, or technologies, for example, could encourage the creation of new sources of income. Services such as basic repairs, special conservation treatments, digitization services, or education and training are several areas where such external work could be productive. Even collection storage, research and development, consultation, and program planning might be appealing for new markets.

Ultimately, success in resource development for preservation and security programs in libraries will be determined by effective education and advocacy with key leaders and funders and also with the user community. We need to inform the administrative and volunteer leadership of our organizations of the impact of preservation and security on learning and scholarship. We need to educate faculty, researchers, students, and community users about responsible use of library collections and also about library commitment to their long-term availability. We need to interest alumni and friends in the significant impact of their financial support for preservation. We should stress its importance to the success of the library and the larger institution. We need to interest vendors in partnering with libraries in the research and development activities that will produce innovative tools for the preservation and security of our collections. And we must encourage new and expanded federal and foundation support for preservation as integral to our national interest.

UNDERSTANDING SUCCESS

Measuring Effectiveness of Preservation and Security Programs

15. Measuring the Effectiveness of Preservation and Security Programs at the Library of Congress

 Francis M. Ponti

Institutions must find accurate and cost-effective ways to assess the effectiveness of their preservation and security programs and to balance access with protection. They need to determine how well controls are working and what needs to be done to correct deficiencies—and then to demonstrate to funders that the money being spent is achieving the stated goals. In large institutions, conducting a full inventory and then periodically measuring changes is often not practicable. Rather, institutions can use statistically valid selection and measuring techniques to estimate the status of the total population of items.

This paper describes different sampling methods and identifies sampling projects undertaken at the Library of Congress. It discusses designing and developing a statistically valid baseline and then using carefully controlled measurements to determine the status of controls in place. Armed with accurate measurements, the institution can make informed decisions about implementing remedies proportional to the risk.

Since its founding, the Library of Congress has been entrusted with the preservation of major works in history, literature, the arts, science, language, and a variety of emerging cultural works. In addition, the Copyright Office function adds hundreds of thousands of works in various formats to the collections each year. The Library staff must find new ways to store, catalog, secure, and preserve many of these works for future generations to come. At the same time, the Library must make its collections relatively open to public observation and use by scholars and private citizens alike. The challenge is to find the balance between these competing goals, namely, preservation and protection versus public accessibility.

Beginning in the 1970s, staff observations and formal studies funded by the Library indicated that public access had resulted in missing materials; defacing of texts, manuscripts, posters, and pictures; and wearing out of materials because of use.

To prevent the first two areas of concern, the Library needed to tighten security and change its methods of serving materials to the public. Library management wanted to be sure that installation of security measures would be done in proportion to the risk involved—but there had to be a balance. Overreaction was to be avoided. For example, it was not feasible to simply close access to most areas. Security experts were consulted, with the result that the security staff was augmented and professionals in the field were hired.

During the 1990s, the Library implemented many innovative security features, several of which involved preventative measures incorporating location and access controls. Other features involved observational and search measures. However, none of these security features pose a major threat to public access.

Installing security and control features can be very costly. The Congress wanted to know whether or not the new security measures were working and, if so, whether or not they were worth the cost. Because much of the cost of security is ongoing, such concerns continue to affect the budget annually.

Measurement of improvement in security and reduction in risk usually involves establishing a baseline and then following up with multiple periods of specific attribute measurements. Some security-minded managers believe that before security features are installed, a baseline wall-to-wall inventory should be taken, followed by another complete inventory in a future period. Making complete inventories for the Library of Congress or for sections within it, however, would be extremely costly and time-consuming. By the time such an inventory was completed, major changes could have taken place, rendering the information from the inventory useless or outdated. The large expenditure of funds would have been wasted.

For almost a century now, business managers in public and private institutions alike have been using quality assurance and control studies involving statistical sampling to save both time and money. When the universe of items to be studied is very large, the institution can use a probability sample of reasonably small size to estimate the condition of that larger universe. With probability selection, we can place reliability bounds on the estimate and provide as precise an estimate as is needed by both management and oversight groups—in the case of the Library, these groups include the General Accounting Office, the Library's Inspector General, and congressional staff. There is an extremely large and varied literature involving the theory and application of statistical sampling to such problems. Both government agencies and universities use these methods. In the Washington, D.C., area, there is no lack of qualified experts in the field.

Sampling with known probabilities of selection allows extrapolation of results to the broader population of items or to locations from which the sample was drawn. Types of sampling plans include:

(1) simple random (equal probability),
(2) stratified random (equal probabilities within subgroups),
(3) cluster or multistage (hierarchical sets of probabilities),
(4) probability proportional to size,
(5) cohort group sampling over time, and
(6) paneled sampling with "births and deaths" over time.

These and other techniques can be tailored to provide efficient and effective measurements with high confidence and precise estimates, but at a much lower cost than a complete inventory of a population. Sampling for measurement of change (because of security or control measures, for example) must also start with a baseline. However, this baseline can be the result of a carefully designed statistical sample. Subsequent samples can then be done over time to measure change within the bounds of statistical significance.

The Library has designed more than a half-dozen sampling plans for its various entities. A few of these plans have been funded, and the results of the testing have been helpful to management in understanding the status of the collections at any given point in time. We were not able to start these samples with a natural baseline at the point where security measures were installed, however, so it is difficult to know the total value of these measurements. If sampling is repeated at regular intervals, management will be able to measure the improvement or deterioration of the collections and evaluate the results in terms either of security control matters or of condition based on normal wear, tear, and deterioration through time.

Because of the lack of a meaningful baseline at the Library in any of its divisions, we had to choose a place to start, with the goal of measuring change through time. We applied sampling techniques to the Prints and Photographs Division and to the National Library Service for the Blind and Physically Handicapped inventory of reading machines for the blind. We were able to study Library holdings for existence and completeness as well as quality. With a baseline, we will be able to measure both quantitative and qualitative benefits of installed controls and security measures. These could then be compared to quantitative and qualitative costs of the installed controls in order to provide the net benefit of the installation and operation of such controls. The key to success in measuring the net benefit is the continuation of sampling and statistical analysis through time.

Although it is true that measurement and testing alone will not fix the problem (actions must be taken and money must be spent to do that), nevertheless such analysis techniques will permit management and oversight authorities to discover and highlight the extent of a problem and the extent of improvement achieved because of actions taken by management.

16. Measuring Environmental Quality in Preservation

James M. Reilly

The purpose of preservation is to safeguard cultural resources for the future without loss of value or usefulness in the present. In practice, this usually means preventing, retarding, or repairing deterioration. Preservation takes many forms, but none is so far-reaching or fundamental as regulation of the storage environment. Here, I will describe new technology from the Image Permanence Institute (IPI) for quantitatively assessing the storage environments of cultural institutions. This new approach is being tested at the Library of Congress in a pilot project to optimize both the quality and the cost of storage environments. The Andrew W. Mellon Foundation funds the project.

A broad definition of the environment encompasses a number of factors that affect the decay of collections, including light, pollution, vibration, radiation, and living organisms. Although all of these are worthy of attention, the two most important environmental factors in preservation are the old stalwarts, temperature and relative humidity (RH). Recent research has yielded an entirely new appreciation of the importance of these two factors in preserving cultural property. Yet the significance of environment transcends preservation. It is also a management issue having profound implications for the fiscal health and long-term success of an institution.

Whether designed for human comfort or for collection preservation, special environments are costly to deliver, all the more so in times of rising energy prices. Environment affects the productivity of staff and the performance of computers and other equipment. Less well appreciated is the fact that the future cultural and market value of collections will be determined by how well they are stored from now on. Better storage will mean less deterioration, which translates into higher future value and decreased costs for repair or reformatting. Managers of cultural institutions need to become more aware of their environmental conditions and to quantify the impact of those conditions on the collections.

The new measures of environmental quality developed by the Image Permanence Institute are based on the effects of storage conditions on the spontaneous decay of organic materials. To understand these conditions, it is necessary to explore the nature of decay processes and the way temperature and RH interact with objects. Temperature and humidity are always present, affecting the collections every minute of every day. Decay can occur through chemical, physical, or biological processes. All three depend heavily on environmental conditions. Biological and physical forms of decay are most influenced by relative humidity, whereas temperature is the critical factor for chemical deterioration. Libraries and archives have the most to fear from chemical decay, because modern information mediums are especially vulnerable to it. The classic example of chemical decay is the yellowing and embrittlement of acidic wood-pulp paper. Paper so weak that the page of a book cannot be turned without breaking has become a familiar sight in libraries around the world. Although the outward manifestation may be physical weakness, the underlying decay process is chemical in nature. Attack on the fibers of the page by acid is a chemical reaction, and, like all chemical reactions, it occurs at a measurable rate, by turns faster or slower depending on conditions.

Considerable scientific inquiry has been made recently into exactly what factors affect the deterioration rate of paper and other organic materials such as plastics, leather, dyes, and textiles—and to what degree. Although the specific problems addressed in the research projects have varied, the results of many of them point to temperature and RH control as the collection manager's best hope. The rate of decay is determined by temperature, concentration, pressure, and the presence or absence of a catalyst. To keep a book from becoming brittle, library managers cannot change the pressure (a constant pressure is provided by the atmosphere) or the presence of an acid catalyst (the papermaker supplied that), but they can regulate concentration and temperature.

Concentration—the amount of each substance involved in a chemical reaction—would seem to be a fixed quantity like atmospheric pressure, but it is not. Although the mass of a book does not change over time, the amount of water absorbed into the book changes with ambient RH. Water plays a direct role in almost every type of chemical decay, so its concentration becomes a primary rate-controlling factor. Ambient RH is therefore an important speed control for chemical deterioration processes. Over the entire range of RH from 0 to 100 percent, the overall rate of chemical decay varies by a factor of ten. The higher the RH, the faster the decay.

Although humidity typically gets the greatest attention from preservation specialists, it is temperature—not humidity—that in fact has the greatest effect on chemical decay. Temperature has the potential to speed up or slow down reaction rates by much more than a factor of ten. A large part of the preservation manager's task is to decide which kind of decay (chemical, physical, or biological) to worry about most. Chemical decay processes are a significant threat to library and archive collections because the information mediums found in libraries are primarily organic in nature and have a high rate of spontaneous decay at room temperature. Microfilm and pictorial films on nitrate and acetate plastic, early sound recordings, color photographs, acid-tanned leather, and acidic papers are but a few examples of such fast-decaying materials. For them, storage at room temperature means they have no hope to survive intact for more than few decades.

Ideas about the durability of library materials have been unconsciously shaped by the apparently good condition of many three- or four-century-old books. But we must bear in mind two key things about the condition of these venerable objects. First, they were made with inherently durable materials, such as parchment, whose life expectancy at room temperature was much longer than many of today's materials. Second, for most of their lives the objects were housed in cooler environments than they typically are housed in now. The low annual average temperature in unheated stone buildings of northern Europe, for example, together with effective means—albeit low-technology methods—to shield them from periods of high humidity, produced a much slower rate of chemical decay than any modern storeroom operated at pleasant and unwavering room temperature. The rare book room kept to tight tolerances at sixty-eight degrees Fahrenheit, 50 percent RH causes the books to deteriorate three to four times faster than their former home in the unheated church or manor house. As a consequence, as much deterioration has occurred in the last fifty years of "good" storage as happened in the previous two centuries.

Most people (including most preservation specialists) underestimate the influence that storage temperature has on the decay rate of organic materials. They underestimate both the negative impact of human comfort temperatures and the magnitude of the benefit gained from going only slightly cooler. Those who would never dream of parting with their home refrigerator or who do not hesitate to condemn as absurd the suggestion that meat-plant workers be allowed to work at room temperature, still maintain that the books, tapes, films, or pictures in their care are just fine at human comfort conditions. The overwhelming weight of scientific evidence says otherwise.

The foundations of IPI's quantitative approach to measuring the effect of environment on the decay rate of organic materials date from the development of predictive accelerated aging methods developed in the 1970s. These test methods were based on principles of physical chemistry and were designed to isolate and characterize the role that temperature plays in the decay of particular materials. As more and more results were published, preservation scientists began to realize the implications of the data and to formulate a larger theoretical framework that brought together both temperature and RH in a unified overview. In the 1980s, Donald Sebera of the Library of Congress created "contour maps" showing what combinations of temperature and RH yielded similar rates of decay for organic materials. He called these maps of equivalent environmental conditions "isoperms." Although this work was an influential and important advance, it did not provide a way to measure the decay rate for varying conditions.

In 1995, the Image Permanence Institute introduced the ability to directly measure and quantify environmental quality, at least as far as natural aging of organic materials is concerned. IPI's TWPI (Time-Weighted Preservation Index) is a way of analyzing temperature and RH data to determine how rapidly or slowly organic materials are decaying because of spontaneous chemical change. An algorithm integrates changing rates into a single number that represents the overall "preservation quality" of a storage environment. The TWPI of a storage space, for example, gives the number of years it would take for a typical "preservation problem" object such as acidic paper to become noticeably deteriorated in a given storage environment. In other words, the TWPI indicates the approximate lifetime of fast-decaying collection materials within that environment. Returning to our example of the rare book room at a constant sixty-eight degrees Fahrenheit, 50 percent RH, its TWPI would be forty-four years. This means that a new book printed on acidic paper would become noticeably deteriorated (discolored and brittle, but not turned into dust) in approximately forty-four years in such an environment.

In recent years, a number of off-site storage spaces have been constructed by major research libraries to relieve overcrowding and offer improved storage conditions. Many of these are designed to operate at around fifty-five degrees Fahrenheit, 35 percent RH. The relative humidity is slowly varied during the course of the seasons so that energy costs are kept to a minimum. The TWPI of such spaces is 163 years, nearly a fourfold improvement over our example above.

The value of the TWPI measurement is that it can integrate changing temperature and RH conditions and deliver one number that reflects the overall quality of the environment. The TWPI can be used to measure existing conditions and to give target figures for optimal conditions, including providing information for cost-benefit analysis of institutional environments. For example, the Library of Congress has used TWPI statistics in planning for its new off-site storage environments.

With funding from the Andrew W. Mellon Foundation, the Image Permanence Institute joined with the Library of Congress in 1999 to explore simultaneously optimizing both the cost of creating collection storage environments and the impact of those storage environments on the longevity of the collections. Working closely with the Preservation Directorate and with the engineering staff of the Architect of the Capitol (the "landlord" of the Library's buildings), IPI is collaborating with the energy-efficiency consulting firm of Herzog/Wheeler and Associates to apply IPI's environmental assessment technology to energy efficiency. Hardware and software developed by IPI will be used in this effort. The Preservation Environment Monitor, a data-logger specially designed for preservation use with funding from the Division of Preservation and Access of the National Endowment for the Humanities (NEH), will be used to gather the data, and Climate Notebook™, a software program created for the purpose of environmental assessment, will be used to perform the analysis of that data.

The project in its second year concentrated on rare book storage areas in the Library's Jefferson Building and manuscript storage areas in the Madison Building. The goals of the project are to double the life expectancy of the collections while simultaneously reducing the consumption of energy. So far, we have collected data to establish a TWPI baseline and have made a close study of the air-conditioning equipment affecting the target areas. Although it is too early to see definitive results from the project, it is already clear that improvements in energy cost and collection longevity are possible. IPI and Herzog/Wheeler will be presenting information to the engineering, preservation, and collection staffs at the Library so that they can determine an optimum combination of human comfort, operating efficiency, and collection preservation. Changes based on these decisions will be implemented, and the project will continue by monitoring and documenting the improvements made. A collateral goal of the project is to describe the management processes during the effort so they can be used by other institutions.

This paper has examined the theory and practice of new environmental quality measures in preservation. These quantifiable measures are the necessary first step toward having an integrated managerial approach to temperature and humidity conditions within cultural institutions. The measures provide a common basis for the engineering, curatorial, and preservation functions to work together toward the larger goals of serving society, maintaining a financially sound program, and enhancing the future value of cultural resource collections.[1]

ELECTRONIC INFORMATION
AND DIGITIZATION
Preservation and Security Challenges

17. Preservation, Security, and Digital Content

 Carl Fleischhauer

Our keywords for this publication—preservation and security—are variously defined, certainly in the context of digital materials. The variation is even greater, and the meanings assigned even broader, when we look at the terms as they are applied to entities in an organization, for example, the "Preservation Department" or the "Security Office." Because this book is about strategic stewardship, I think that it is fitting to discuss things from an organizational perspective and to take a broader view.

Let me say a few words about the first term, "preservation." For illustration, allow me to oversimplify a bit about the old days, when our concern was focused exclusively on physical objects. Let us take books, for instance. Preservation departments within libraries were organized to conserve the books and—when necessary—to reformat them (which usually meant microfilming them). If thought was given to adding intellectual value, this was seen as the business of other units within the library, perhaps where a selection process assembled the collection, where cataloging took place, or where the reference staff placed materials in the hands of readers.

Added intellectual value was a matter of providing a context for a given item within a larger, cataloged collection. And the collection itself had intellectual value: the whole was greater than the sum of the parts.

With digital activities, we have seen organizational boundaries begin to weaken. The Library of Congress program called American Memory is a classic—but by no means the only—example of a reformatting project motivated by the desire to expand access.[1] Such activities reproduce the original objects and at the same time add intellectual value by improving access, especially when they produce searchable texts. Here, even the parts are "greater" than they were before digitization.

I know that the reproductions in American Memory are often described as access-quality copies, but the program and allied efforts at the Library of Congress have also investigated copy-making in the service of preservation. (Please note that we use the term "preservation copy" at the Library of Congress even when we retain the original item.) For some types of material, we have begun to produce very high-quality reproductions. The digital images produced by the Geography and Map Division, for example, surpass in quality the 105mm microfiche traditionally produced for the division, and the paper output from the scans far and away surpasses any output obtainable from the film. I am not sure if the division has started using the p-word for their digital copies, but the images certainly fill the same niche that analog preservation copies used to fill.

Meanwhile, the Prints and Photographs Division is starting to hear from publishers who are well satisfied with the uncompressed master images they download from the Web, suggesting that here, too, digital images can take the place of what were called preservation copy negatives. At the Library of Congress and elsewhere, we are impressed by the effective service to researchers that is offered by, say, color images of manuscript pages. Such digital images are susceptible to enlargement and improvements in legibility when examined using well-selected software. (Alas, audio and video lag behind in terms of online quality, but I am convinced they will catch up soon.)

In the face of these developments, the people who are developing digital reformatting programs have moved from discussing the basics to discussing the niceties. When should we reproduce a book's pages as ink imprints, that is, capture what amounts to be the typography and lines in drawings? This approach permits us to create clean paper facsimiles, as demonstrated by the Cornell University library scanning projects of the 1990s. Alternatively, when shall we make images of the pages that use a photographic approach to capture the look of the sheets (including paper color) in the manner demonstrated by Octavo CD-ROM editions of rare volumes?[2] When is it important to conserve the original bound volume even in the face of lower image quality? Are there ever times when the circumstances dictate disbinding a book in order to make perfect facsimile images? And, to echo my earlier remarks, this question: for this body of material, how shall we add value and improve access? This last topic is now understood to include not only options like exchangeable MARC (MAchine-Readable Cataloging) catalog records, but also standardized finding aids, searchable full texts, and "exposing and harvesting" the detailed, local data that live in intimate relationships with digitized content.

The Library of Congress has only just begun to examine the parallel set of issues for "born-digital" content. To some degree, the added intellectual value will come—as in the past —from assembling and cataloging a collection and providing access to it. The challenge of distributed custody—the likelihood that digital content will be held by different libraries or publisher-owners—will be met by the development of refined conventions for describing and indexing this dispersed content.

What does all this mean for libraries and archives? One answer is drawn from an organizational model in which an office or a family of related offices tackles a mix of issues: first, making reproductions, the reformatting aspect of preservation; second, analyzing and processing born-digital content; third, contributing to the addition of intellectual value by various means; and fourth, preserving content once in digital form, the other aspect of preservation, presumably including the value-added elements. I will note here an interesting discussion we are having at the Library, working to distinguish the role of keeper of the digital content from the role of shaper and indexer of the digital content for end-user access.

What can we say about preserving content in digital form? Solutions are beginning to emerge. Different methods will be applied depending on whether we are talking about the content in a library's custody or the content for which a library takes responsibility but does not have custody. The latter—what the National Library of Australia calls "remote management"—is out of scope for this discussion. It is worth mentioning, however, that the preservation of remote resources will include certifying custodians and binding them in legal agreements. The former, however, is the question we address here: how will we preserve that which is in our custody?

One key element is covered by the broad term "security." A recent report from the National Research Council notes that security has conventionally encompassed secrecy, confidentiality, integrity, and availability.[3] Using the broad term "trustworthiness," the report adds other terms or, as the report puts it, other "dimensions": correctness, reliability, privacy, safety, and survivability. The report notes that the dimensions are not independent: to increase one (say, confidentiality) will inevitably decrease another (availability). Information technology professionals know that it is difficult to manage these dimensions in a networked environment in which many software applications are commercial packages produced by third parties.

Consideration of security—or trustworthiness—leads organizations to hone their skills in a family of actions. Many operational and administrative components must be brought together to provide a trustworthy networked environment. In my conversations with colleagues at the Library of Congress, I have started to hear what amounts to a checklist of these components:

(1) ensure the physical security of buildings, hardware, and cabling;

(2) install and integrate firewalls and routers to control network traffic;

(3) authenticate users and authorize their access to appropriate zones within the institution's systems;

(4) protect the integrity of systems and data against corruption caused by accident, errors, or infiltration by unauthorized persons;

(5) monitor data integrity;

(6) monitor network traffic;

(7) back up systems and data and establish disaster recovery plans; and

(8) develop guidelines for individual users and train them in the use of these guidelines.

The trustworthiness that will result from assembling these components will provide a necessary—but not sufficient—condition for the preservation of content. Several commentators have summarized the known approaches to preserving digital content in five categories, at least two of which are addressed by a trustworthy networked information system: (1) refreshing the bits and (2) using better media. "Refreshing" refers to copying a stream of bits from one location to another, whether the physical medium is the same or not, to keep the bits alive without change. "Better media" refers to the longevity and technology-independence of storage media, which may be more important for offline than for online storage.

As an aside, I will confess that I do not quite know the best location for "authenticity" in this cyber-geography. Like many others, I have been impressed by the papers on this topic resulting from the Council on Library and Information Resources discussion in January 2000.[4] But the papers demonstrate that the issues are too numerous to permit easy resolution. "Authentic" in what sense? If authenticity is a matter of a document's properties, do we mean all properties or just some properties? To what degree is the need met by technological elements: checksums, encryption, signatures? How shall we distinguish the elements pertaining to "integrity" from those pertaining to "authenticity"? Cliff Lynch's paper in this volume reminds us of our dependence on "trust," especially trust in an intermediary to whom we turn to authenticate a document.[5]

Let me leave authenticity to those better able to explain it and return to the five digital-content preservation categories. I mentioned (1) refreshing the bits and (2) using better media, associating them with security and trustworthiness. The truth is, one could define the term "trustworthiness" to cover the next three categories as well: (3) migration of content, (4) emulation of the technical environment, and (5) digital paleography. Migration includes the transformation of content from one data representation (digital format) to another, that is, from one digital format for images (say, TIFF, or tagged image file format) to a future standard format that provides enhanced functionality. Emulation requires that one use the power of a new generation of technology to function as if it were the technology of a previous generation. For example, the provision of future access to the computer game *Myst* would almost certainly require the emulation of Windows 95 (the Microsoft operating system released in 1995) and other elements. Peter Hirtle's definition of "digital paleography" alludes to "the venerable science and art of reading and deciphering old or obscure handwriting." Hirtle envisions digital paleographers who can, say, read files encoded in HTML 1.0 (the first version of Hypertext Markup Language) and convert them to "whatever standard may then be current, be it XML [Extensible Markup Language] and a stylesheet, a hand-held markup language, or an eBook standard."[6]

How might we accomplish migration or emulation? (I cannot think of a thing to say about digital paleography.) One answer is to seize the moment when content first arrives at our door or when we create it in a reformatting program. This is our best opportunity to be sure we have a preservable digital object. An analogy may be drawn with preservable physical objects. We seek to acquire physical books bound in signatures and printed on acid-free paper, knowing that they are inherently easier to conserve than cheaply bound volumes printed on acidic paper. We produce preservation microfilm on polyester-based film and process it according to preservation standards in the laboratory. By the same token, we will wish to acquire born-digital books with texts in an accepted markup language and illustrations in standard image file formats. Such items will be inherently easier to migrate than electronic books with texts and illustrations in proprietary formats that require special software for viewing. Or—in the case of an eBook in a proprietary structure that provides valuable "behavior"—the most preservable electronic instance will be one that is accompanied by thorough documentation and tools to maximize playability as computer systems change. Everyone agrees that these circumstances cry out for special metadata: we need information about the form and structure of the content, about the systems that might have to be emulated to play it, about access restrictions, and more. We need technical metadata to support migration, emulation, or a judicious combination of the two.

It is worth a word about "look and feel" or "object behavior" in these examples. Reformatting (which can be viewed as a type of migration) transforms the look and feel of the physical book: a microfilm has no pages to turn, no paper to touch, just frames to advance. Similarly, we can expect some change in the look and feel of the migrated cyber book as next-generation software renders the text in a different way, or a new, higher resolution display screen or printer renders the illustration at reduced size. We trust that these changes will be minor—I do not quite dare say "aesthetic"—and that the information contained by text and picture will remain intact. In contrast, the look and feel of the non-migratable cyber book—or a book for which a curator is willing to pay the price to maintain its look and feel—will remain unchanged as long as system emulation can be provided. Although experts differ on this, we worry that the level of effort required to accomplish emulation will be greater than the effort needed to migrate, when migration is possible. As one of my colleagues points out, it may be easier to apply methods for searching an extended digital corpus at any given time if that corpus has been migrated into newer formats.

Reformatting programs make cyber objects that reproduce original physical items. At the Library of Congress, the general strategy for digital reformatting has been to produce migratable content, that is, reproductions of the originals and an object structure designed to permit migration. These reproductions are structured to provide a representation of the original item that is as good as or better than conventional re-formatted copies. These copies must be at least as good as a microfilm's representation of a book or an analog audio tape's representation of a wax cylinder. In no case are these reproductions intended to emulate the complete look and feel or behavior of the original items. But there is an opportunity here to add value of a different sort, as in the case of rendering the text in searchable form.

What is a library's role when others are the makers of the objects? The event of acquiring offers a useful point of consideration, representing as it does the transaction between a library and the maker or the maker's representative. At this point, there may be an opportunity—as has been the case with the push for the use of acid-free paper in book manufacturing—to influence makers to produce digital content in more preservable form. The desire to influence makers has special meaning for the Library of Congress, where some acquisitions result from the workings of the copyright law. In these instances, the Library can define "best editions" (the form of a work desired by the Library for its collections) in ways that are most supportive of content preservation. The acquisition event is also a moment for the analysis of arriving digital content and the documentation of the features that are relevant for preservation planning. It may also be a moment for carrying out a cost-benefit analysis that weighs one preservation approach against another.

What do these ideas mean for the institution and its organization? Earlier, I alluded to an office or offices that would make reproductions, add intellectual value, and preserve content in digital form. But if digital content preservation entails operating a trustworthy networked information system, migrating content, and emulating systems, to say nothing of analysis-upon-acquisition and the execution of legal agreements for remote resources—well, we are surely not talking about an office in the singular. This calls for distributed responsibilities and carries a strong need for computer science expertise. Come to think of it, I guess this begins to describe a library in a digital age. It reminds us that securing and preserving digital content require a collective effort that will depend on the contributions of many people.

18. The Coming Crisis in Preserving Our Digital Cultural Heritage

Clifford A. Lynch

This paper offers a brief survey and synthesis of several developments in areas as diverse as intellectual property law, the marketplace for cultural and intellectual goods, and the technologies involved in maintaining digital information across long periods of time. These developments are converging to create a crisis in our ability to preserve our cultural heritage as this heritage increasingly migrates into digital formats.

In the historical period we are just leaving behind, the stewardship of cultural and intellectual heritage was primarily concerned with the acquisition and subsequent preservation of physical artifacts. Copies of books, sound recordings, photographs, prints, pamphlets, and other materials were made available in the public marketplace. (There was also, of course, a market in original unique objects such as paintings, but this involves different issues, which I do not consider in this paper.) Libraries and other institutions concerned with preserving our heritage obtained copies through purchase, donation, or other means and then kept the artifacts in trust for society. Anything broadly available commercially or for free was available to libraries as well as to individuals. This was enabled by a legal framework that included both copyright law and the doctrine of first sale.

There were of course problems. Some artifacts offered in the marketplace were poorly constructed for long-term persistence, for instance, books printed on acid paper; the intent of the producers was inexpensive mass production for a consumer market. Some important cultural materials were not sold as artifacts, and libraries had trouble obtaining copies, as has been the case with television broadcasts or films before the emergence of the videocassette marketplace. Other artifacts could be used only with technical playback systems that quickly became obsolete or unavailable, for instance, early computer games and some audio and video materials. In an ironic twist of fate, the only surviving record we have of many early films is the paper prints that were deposited for copyright registration in 1894 and the following decades. The films themselves were produced for limited distribution on volatile nitrate film stock that is long gone, and the studios that created them often did not even try to preserve them; indeed, many early studios simply went out of business. But the system worked well enough—particularly for print and sound recordings, where a mass market existed from the beginning. Libraries were able to have access to the vast majority of our cultural and intellectual heritage and to select what they wished to preserve from this treasure trove, and our civilization is immeasurably richer for this.

More and more of our society's new cultural and intellectual works are being produced in digital forms. Older works are also being repackaged (sometimes with important enhancements) as digital products. As this migration takes place, we are seeing the emergence of a new and very different marketplace in intellectual and cultural goods. In this new marketplace, content is moving to disembodied collections of bits that are delivered over the network, removed from any specific artifactual "carrier." Even in the still-numerous transitional cases where carrier media remain in use, the complexity and rate of obsolescence of the playback system technology mean that it will become increasingly commonplace to find media that can no longer be played. There are relatively short windows of opportunity when content can be copied and reformatted from one medium to another while old and new playback technologies briefly coexist in the marketplace. Preservation requires active management and continual vigilance.

The terms of availability are changing as well. Rather than selling an artifact, content is made available to the public under constrained license terms that restrict sharing, copying, transfer of ownership, display, performance, and other use, sometimes far beyond the customary constraints imposed on artifacts by copyright law. In the most extreme cases, consumers do not obtain works at all, but rather the right to experience a work for a limited time under a pay-per-view or similar rental framework, with no guarantee that a work enjoyed today will still be available to be enjoyed tomorrow, even if the reader is prepared to pay the additional fees. These "pay-per-view" arrangements convert a much larger class of works than the traditional performing arts into ephemeral, transient, experiential things that sometimes may only be shared or revisited through memory and re-description rather than through revisiting the work itself.

Content that is available to the consumer may simply not be available to libraries under terms that allow long-term retention and future provision to the interested public. Although there has never been an obligation on the part of publishers and other content distributors to accommodate libraries among their customers (and thus ensure that their materials will be available to the society for the long term) as part of marketing their wares to the general public, in an era characterized by a marketplace in artifacts, it was very hard to avoid doing so.

In the new world of digital content and commerce governed by license, it is very easy to target experiential consumer markets while explicitly excluding long-term access (ownership of copies) either by private collectors or by cultural heritage institutions such as libraries. This shift is well illustrated by the new characterization of music as a "service" that is being promoted by some parts of the recording industry. Rather than acquiring ownership of copies of specific musical works, consumers pay for a subscription that allows them to listen on demand to a large but perhaps ever-changing corpus of music, the details of which are determined by the industry. This may be attractive to the consumer, but it is problematic for organizations concerned with the long-term preservation of the cultural record.

We are still limited in what we know about either the costs or the best technical strategies for preserving digital content. In particular, we face difficult intellectual issues about exactly what we are trying to preserve. But we are developing a broad consensus in several areas. First, we need to focus on the bits, and not the artifacts that may temporarily carry them. The bits that define the works—and not the media that may house the bits at any given time—are what are important and what need to be preserved. In a world of short-lived artifacts and even shorter-lived playback systems, we cannot count on bits stored on and bound to artifacts to be reliably readable in the long term simply because we have placed the artifacts on shelves. Instead, the strategy is to copy bits from older storage technologies to newer ones on a continuous basis, taking advantage of those periods when generations of technologies overlap and copying can be done inexpensively, and without incurring the risks involved in making assumptions about the shelf-life of the various media. Preservation of digital materials is a continuous, active process (requiring steady funding), rather than a practice of benignly neglecting artifacts stored in a hospitable environment, perhaps punctuated by interventions every few decades for repairs.

Second, we recognize that maintaining bits in a digital world depends not only on storage hardware but also on software to interpret the bits and that software systems and standards (image, audio, and video formats, for example) will evolve over time. Because of this, not only do we need to simply copy bits, but we also periodically need to reformat works from older standards to newer ones to ensure that we will continue to have available software that can interpret the bits. Whereas we know a great deal about the mechanics of how to manage bits across time, we have no general theory of how to manage the migration of formats across time as standards and software evolve, though there is some basis for optimism about our ability to successfully navigate format migrations case by case assuming we are able to ensure that digital materials receive sustained and careful attention and stewardship. This is the best understanding we have today about preserving digital information, along with a well-honed sense of the fragility of complex digital information such as interactive computer games or simulations that depend not just on rendering content for the human perceptual system but on the integral participation of computing systems in mediating the "performance" or execution of the digital work.

Third and last, we have learned that preserving digital works is difficult, even if we can easily read all the bits when the work first arrives at the archive that is to manage it, and even if the format of the work is well documented. But we are facing disturbing developments that make the task of preservation infinitely more difficult. Some works are no longer available in the marketplace as open, documented files of bits. Rather, they are encrypted and wrapped in protective active software systems that perform and enforce rights management by preventing copying. New laws (discussed below) have made it a crime to attempt to bypass these protections (though there are some exemptions), but even leaving aside the legal issues, these protective measures vastly complicate the copying and reformatting that is necessary to preserve digital works.

It is probably not an exaggeration to say that the most fundamental problem facing cultural heritage institutions is the ability to obtain digital materials together with sufficient legal rights to be able to preserve these materials and make them available to the public over the long term. Without explicit and affirmative permissions from the rights-holders, this is likely to be impossible. Such permission is no longer part of the standard commercial framework as we have moved toward licensing and pay-per-view agreements and away from a marketplace dominated by long-lived artifacts. Indeed, recent legal developments—in particular, some of the provisions of the Digital Millennium Copyright Act, such as those dealing with anticircumvention—have made it much more difficult for libraries to act to preserve digital content in the absence of explicit permissions from rights-holders. Legislation such as the Uniform Computer Information Transaction Act (UCITA) has helped to legitimize pay-per-view and licensing frameworks. The Sonny Bono Copyright Extension Act, by stretching out the term of copyright, has also made libraries more dependent on obtaining explicit permissions to ensure that digital materials are preserved for the long term. Because of the new, extraordinarily long terms of copyright, it is even more improbable that artifacts bearing digital content, or the digital content itself, will remain readable throughout the duration of copyright without active stewardship.

In this new world, then, content may not be preserved by traditional cultural memory institutions, except perhaps by the Library of Congress, by virtue of its special, peculiar status, under American copyright deposit (and the issues here are not entirely clear at present), or by other national libraries under their own national copyright deposit arrangements, unless the rights-holders take steps to make sure that this happens. This prospect places a heavy burden on these national libraries and is particularly dangerous because of the high degree of reliance on a handful of unique institutions that are subject to the vagaries of politically based funding and policy direction. The preservation of large portions of our cultural heritage may depend critically on ample and consistent annual funding to a single institution. A few years of budget austerity could cause large portions of this record to vanish. Previously, for print collections, a wide range of public and private funding sources underwrote the preservation of the record, and the nature of preserving print was such that it could survive considerable periods of lean budgets. An equally diverse group of institutions both public and private (as well as individual collectors) actually collected and preserved the materials, and these materials are widely distributed.

We have several sets of issues to consider as we look beyond the possible special role of the national libraries, which can invoke copyright deposit regulations as a means of obtaining control of copies of materials for preservation. (Note that there is a broader, and much more complex and controversial issue involved here, which is largely beyond the scope of this paper: who gets access to the materials and under what terms? The problem is one of finding a balance that does not destroy the marketplace in cultural and intellectual goods, but that still provides some measure of access to the public through cultural memory organizations. Negotiating this balance will be an extraordinary challenge. I am focusing here more narrowly on preservation.) If the broader community of libraries, archives, museums, universities, and other cultural heritage institutions is to exercise stewardship over our intellectual record in the digital age, as matters stand today these institutions will need to obtain permissions to perform these functions. How and why might they obtain such permissions?

For publishers in the consumer marketplace, the concerns are with revenue maximization and asset management through managed availability. At best, questions of long-term preservation of their wares as cultural heritage are irrelevant (think about broadcasts of the nightly news, or about newspapers migrating to the digital medium). At worst, it runs actively counter to their economic interests (here, think about entertainment products like music). To be clear, there is growing recognition that archives of various materials do have economic value, and many content producers are offering products that involve archives (such as the newspaper industry); but this is changing content into new products, not preserving it for the longer term when it is no longer viable as a product. It is not at all clear why these content-owners—particularly the smaller or newer organizations that have not yet become cultural institutions in their own right—will even bother to spend the time and money to engage the issues of putting permissions in place to ensure preservation, much less actually grant the needed permissions.

There is another large class of content that can best be termed "ephemera"—network-based analogs of pamphlets, broadsides, menus, transportation schedules, and the like. Historically, if libraries could obtain a copy of such items, they could preserve them using the framework of copyright, but for current materials, legal agreements and permissions are needed. Yet the authors of these works are often not major economic players, or they produce content as a byproduct of other economic activities; they do not have the funding or the interest to enter into such legal agreements. Indeed, it is often impossible even to identify the authors of such works or to engage them in a discussion about such agreements. One can see this problem vividly in the efforts of the Internet Archive, which simply collects publicly accessible Web pages on a continuing basis and archives them under what are at best uncertain legal auspices. The notion of the Internet Archive actually negotiating with the author of each Web site and obtaining permission to make, store, and maintain a copy of the site is literally unthinkable.

In the old world of physical artifacts, simply by publishing their works so that an archive or library could obtain a copy, authors would in effect enter into the necessary agreements to ensure that their works would be archived as a byproduct, but this is no longer the case. The category of ephemera is actually very broad—consider advertising, for example—and grows ever broader as more people employ the Web as a democratic, low-barrier-to-entry means of sharing their ideas. Access to the digital printing press has truly become available to almost everyone, but without the historic properties that accompanied the physical output of the older printing press that were so essential to preservation.

It is informative to look at the case of academic and scholarly journals that have moved to the digital world. This is a very different situation than we find in the consumer marketplace. Here, in most cases, libraries constitute the primary marketplace. But even more to the point, these journals exist to serve their authors and readers, who are scholars operating within a strong culture of the importance of maintaining the intellectual record. Organizations such as the Coalition for Networked Information, the Council on Library and Information Resources, and the Association of Research Libraries have sponsored a number of meetings over the past few years to try to address issues of archiving scholarly journals of record as they move to digital form. One very strong message that has emerged from these discussions is that there is a deeply held shared commitment to archiving and to the integrity of the intellectual record as represented by these publications. The publishers of these works, by and large, have made it clear that they are prepared to assign the necessary rights and permissions to libraries to ensure that these works are archived and maintained for the long term. They understand that they have an obligation to do so in order to keep faith with their authors and readers, and that if they do not do so, they will not be able to continue to attract authors and readers as their publications migrate to digital form. Even if they were unwilling to do this, it seems likely that libraries, as their primary customers, could persuade them to do so, but such market pressure appears to be largely unnecessary. There is a shared, common set of values that says that preservation is essential and that the appropriate permissions simply must be put in place to make it happen.

Some difficult technical, economic, and organizational issues need to be resolved in order to put an effective and comprehensive system of archiving for scholarly journals of record in place. And yet, these developments—and, most particularly, this strong affirmation of common values related to the integrity and preservation of the intellectual record—leave me optimistic that the problems will be solved.

But contrast this to mass market cultural products. We have little evidence so far that creators, consumers, and publishers in this world have been able to articluate a similar set of shared values around preservation. Many rights–holders are keen on the notion that they can simply withdraw a work from circulation at will, regardless of how many people may have seen it and the extent of the work's impact on society. As discussed already, there is a new emphasis on content that is offered only on a limited-time and limited-use basis rather than having copies distributed for continued consideration and reassessment. And, of course, the impact of a work and its cultural value may be perceived only in retrospect. Orwellian scenarios involving the purging or rewriting of what is clearly well-established cultural and intellectual history are actually embraced by some as desirable and even attractive consequences of the new technologies of content control and the new licensing frameworks.

The issues in question are actually quite profound and nuanced intellectually, and it is not clear what the right answers are. We have traditions of creators as owners, enjoying the exercise of both property and moral rights over their creations. But offsetting this, for example, we have a strong historical tradition that considers publication an essentially irrevocable act, that once a work is published, it cannot be withdrawn from the public record. As a society, we generally reject government censorship and are at best deeply uncomfortable with the idea that the exercise of ownership rights can reverse the act of publication rather than amend it. In this tradition, it may be possible to prevent new copies from entering the hands of the public, reducing the work to a rare and specialized, but not inaccessible part of that public record. The work becomes something that may be consulted, perhaps with some difficulty or inconvenience, without necessarily being available in new copies for new purchase. In effect, our cultural and intellectual record has been supplied by the consumer marketplace over time but has existed distinct and independent from the present status of that marketplace at any particular point in time. Rather, the cultural record has represented a summation of all that has ever been available in the marketplace.

Today, in a radically altered legal and technical landscape, it appears possible to change all this—but should we, and if so, on what basis? Libraries and other cultural heritage organizations have traditionally served as the society's advocates for preservation. One can all too readily envision futile attempts by these cultural heritage organizations to intervene in the new consumer marketplaces, where content is made available only on a pay-per-view basis. Libraries simply do not represent a significant sector of the marketplace, and they are likely to be told either to accept the same terms as every other consumer or to refrain from licensing the product if they do not like the terms—or even that the distributor of the work simply does not care to do business with libraries at all. If this disenfranchising of our cultural heritage institutions, this elimination of any opportunity to preserve these materials, occurs, it will hurt our society in the long term. Such an issue is unlikely to be resolved by marketplace forces.

It is all too easy to invoke a sort of narrow legal and economic determinism here, to simply say that our current laws and marketplaces empower the rights-holder (and even perhaps the consumer) and that this is a good thing. We may be tempted to make vague references to the inevitability and necessity of the globalization and harmonization of intellectual property law or to argue the economic need to maintain parity with European Community copyright law and policy, all as a way of abdicating any real responsibility for social consequences. Standing in opposition to these developments, but too often overlooked today, is the fundamental constitutional construction of intellectual property in American society.

Intellectual property rights are not just another form of property rights, they are a part of a pact between creators and society as a whole. These rights are a tool to advance the "sciences and useful arts," as specified in the U.S. Constitution. Rights are assigned for a limited term, with the intent that after that term, works will become part of a national intellectual patrimony, a part of the public domain.

As I understand it, the Constitution does not speak directly to a public intellectual and cultural record, though copyright deposit legislation looks to the ongoing construction of such a record. And surely such a record is vital, not only as precursor to the public domain but also as a necessary prerequisite for an informed, educated, accountable, vital, and democratic society. Our society, at least as we conceive of it today, needs its libraries and its intellectual and cultural record. Perhaps the framers of the Constitution saw such a record as a thing that would evolve and thrive naturally and hence needed only limited protection through provisions such as the freedom of the press (though certainly our ideas about how broad, and how public, such a record should be has expanded since the writing of the Constitution, and has developed in tandem with the evolution of democratic cultural heritage institutions such as public museums and libraries). Perhaps the framers could not foresee the constellation of economic, technical, and legal forces that today is assembling to threaten the existence and integrity of such a record, and thus felt no need to build in explicit protection against these forces. This is an area where constitutional, legal, political, historical, and cultural scholars are shaping the discussion that we need to have.

Interestingly, the risks we suffer are not those of direct government control over the intellectual record. The vision that George Orwell portrayed in *1984* (to cite one canonical example from a rich genre) was of a totalitarian government that had obtained comprehensive control over this record and that continually rewrote it in order to maintain power and to further its own ends. What is threatening us today is not an abuse of centralized power, but rather a low-key, haphazard deterioration of the intellectual and cultural record that is driven primarily by economic motivations and the largely unintended and unforeseen consequences of new intellectual property laws that were enacted at the behest of powerful commercial interests and in the context of new and rapidly evolving technologies.

It is time for a blunt, fundamental discussion about the importance of preserving our social, cultural, and intellectual heritage as a key public policy goal; about the need to maintain this as a record that is held in trust for all citizens and that can be consulted by all citizens. We need to explore if and how to formalize new principles: for example, once a work has influenced the thinking of millions of people, it must, at some level, become part of the heritage of society as a whole, and we as citizens must have some rights and capabilities to revisit it. In other words, there is a point at which works that reach the public must become in some sense part of a public record. We need to be clear about how the social and intellectual record differs from the marketplace in intellectual properties and the extent to which this record is permitted to encroach upon the unfettered operation of the marketplace. And perhaps, in order to encourage the development and maintenance of this record, we need to make it easy for ephemera to enter this record and subsequently to be preserved without special actions on the part of creators. We need to consider whether restrictions on use or easy incorporation into the public record, and later the public domain, should be the default mode of operation in the absence of specific, affirmative actions by creators or their agents.

But we also need to be absolutely clear that the social and intellectual record at issue here is not necessarily something that is available instantly, without charge, and without limitation from any computer connected to the Internet; it is something that is held in trust, collectively, by our cultural memory institutions. We must still address the exquisitely complex and delicate problem of how we can provide at least some level of access to this record (and what levels of access to what part of the record) without damaging the marketplace that creates so much of its vibrancy and richness.

A particular group of questions to which we must be sensitive concern the rights of authors and other creators, as distinct from the rights of publishers and other large corporate entities that often present themselves as speaking on behalf of creators. My focus here is not primarily economic; on an economic basis there is often considerable alignment between authors and publishers, and the central issue I am concerned with here is what can be preserved, not the ability of authors to derive income from a marketplace in their works. The most recent revisions of American copyright law have begun to introduce European notions of "moral" rights of creators into the discussion, in part because of international harmonization. At least in theory, the new legal and technical capabilities give creators (or their assignees) an unprecedented ability to withdraw their works from circulation or otherwise control how they are seen after publication—or perhaps more appropriately, after they are granted broad availability, because the idea of publication per se seems to be ever more elusive. The fear is that moral rights will not be invoked by creators to protect the integrity of their works, but that they will become the tool of other interests in manipulating availability for other ends.

There are many kinds of creators with many purposes. A poet no longer comfortable with his or her youthful published works and who would just as soon see them forgotten is very different from someone now nominated for high office who is haunted by an embarrassing speech from a few years past that he or she would like to expunge from the record before the news media can obtain copies. Both of these cases are in turn very different from investigations of attempts to manipulate the price of stocks over time through the message-board discourse that has developed among investors in the digital world. Although all of these might be grouped together under a legalistic analysis, I think that the public would have very different degrees of sympathy for the rights of the creator to withdraw his or her works from public scrutiny from one scenario to another. The correct answers here are anything but clear because of this enormous variation, but the questions need to be part of our conversation about the future of the intellectual record, particularly in conjunction with the possible emergence of technologies that can "undo" publication or other broad distribution.

The recent *Tasini v. New York Times et al.* litigation is an excellent illustration of some of the issues and dilemmas that we must face in addressing the maintenance of an effective intellectual and cultural record in digital form as a public policy goal, and of balancing this goal with the rights of creators. The *Tasini* case also illustrates the problems of sheer scale, of practicality, and of overhead and transaction costs that may arise in trying to honor creators' rights as we try to migrate much of our existing cultural record to digital form in a context of extremely lengthy terms of copyright protection. It is somewhat different from the other situations I have discussed but has important resonances.

In *Tasini* we have a situation where the courts found that a number of authors have suffered an injustice. Their rights to control and benefit from the use of their works have not been respected. But redressing these abuses could have a high social cost: the potential corruption of key parts of our intellectual record. These authors contributed materials to major newspapers and magazines of record that were read by millions, and their works were reproduced in digital representations of these publications of record, thus providing an accurate digital representation of record that reflected the earlier printed works. The authors argued—and the courts agreed—that because the publishers did not have the rights to supply their works for inclusion in these digital compendia, their works should now be removed unless the publishers come to terms with the authors and obtain their permissions. Pragmatically, it presents a real problem for the publishers: there are many authors involved and many works involved, and simply contacting all of them and concluding the necessary negotiations is a huge—perhaps impossible—task. Many database providers have removed substantial numbers of articles from their databases as a result of the decision. The only good news here is that although the integrity of the digital record has been damaged, we still have print and microform copies of the original newspapers to refer to (however inconvenient this may be).

We must find ways to avoid such debacles in future, particularly when we may no longer have the earlier print record as a recourse.

The public policy discussion needs to focus on questions about what sort of intellectual and cultural record we need to maintain, and why, and what authorizations are necessary to assemble and maintain this record and to protect its integrity. Legal issues—including perhaps the need for new legislation, or for changes to existing legislation—should follow from these broader public policy goals. We should not allow the existing legal frameworks and marketplace practices to overly constrain our thinking about what goals are possible or desirable. We must not let the public debate be dominated by technical legal issues about the interpretation of currently existing legislation. The digital age will be very different, and some key laws on the books today have been enacted very early in the transition to this digital age. Our understanding, insight, and wisdom about the nature of a digital world are naturally and necessarily limited. Some of those laws—for example, the Digital Millennium Copyright Act—are already producing what many believe are undesirable and unintended consequences as we begin to see their first applications in actual cases.

One thing is clear. Without such a public policy debate

and the changes that may occur as a result of it, by simply letting existing legal and marketplace forces continue to operate along their current trajectory, we may face a crisis in our ability to capture and preserve our cultural and intellectual record in the emerging digital age. Future scholars may look back at the early years of the twenty-first century as a dark age, where we find we have irrevocably lost much of our cultural memory because libraries and other cultural heritage organizations could no longer function effectively, and indeed even individual collectors of intellectual and cultural works, who have often historically served as a safety net for libraries, had lost much of their ability to build and keep collections. And these future scholars may also recognize a society in the early twenty-first century as deeply troubled by a loss of accountability and of intellectual and artistic continuity and haunted by recurrent bouts of amnesia about the basis and nature of its own activities and actions. A systemic failure of our cultural heritage institutions is likely to exact a real price on the society overall, not just on our commitment to the importance of scholarly inquiry.

19. Electronic Information and Digitization · *Preservation and Security Challenges*

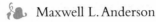 Maxwell L. Anderson

Museum and library professionals have always assumed that preservation of the evidence of the past is their primary responsibility, but that long-held assumption is now being tested by the advent of digital media. This paper will consider obstacles and solutions ahead for administrators who seek to preserve intellectual property in digital form, with an emphasis on museums and libraries. The three main obstacles such administrators confront are: our instinctive devotion to preserving all artworks and intellectual property at any cost, the instability of a digital platform, and the fluid and seemingly infinite permutations of any digital experience.

Institutional fetishism is our first dilemma. Art has been at the core of human prehistory and history. But a heretical question is posed in the contemporary world: would we be better off now if it had been possible for the entire record of past creativity to have been preserved? The question is more urgent given today's creative explosion through the chip and the network, in an age in which every banal whispered sentiment or retinally scanned visual bitstream stands ready to be uploaded to a personal Web page, to float in an unfathomably vast ether of data. The curator's spirit of advocacy is the first problem we face, and the Solomonic decisions that await us are more complicated than ever because of the sheer volume of creativity to be charted in a digital world. Complicating the situation even further, this digital transformation is happening at a time when the relativistic fashions of the academy have made art historians and critics resistant to defining hierarchies of quality. Yet, taste and critical judgment to decide what will survive have never been more in demand.

Digital artists today work in a way that defies the conservator's impulse to protect. Possible permutations of the digital experience are so numerous that it is not feasible for any individual or group to determine which are the best suited to our attentions. Conservators need curators to define which are the works most deserving of perpetuation. The impulse of the day from the keyboard of the artist is not to be explicit about what is the preferred context of experiencing digital art; artists invoke instead a "do-it-yourself" spirit that reduces the authority of the artist and engages the participation of the broad public. Like many academics, the artists themselves eschew the role of arbiter of how their art is to be experienced. Neither do they look to curators to decide this question. Although the conservation of a screen capture is a complicated enterprise unto itself, the screen capture is hardly a compelling version of a work of Internet art, and it is often the interactivity of a Web site that gives the work meaning, rather than a series of static pages.

The core problem in this preservation dilemma remains the simple one of volume. Of all that is available, who is to decide what is worth preserving? Artists who use digital video and the Internet as their media are increasingly a self-reliant lot, for whom the museum is a curmudgeonly, old-guard institution insisting on antiquated methods of display. The presentation of streaming video is not like the display of a painting. Here there is notionally no reason to make room for other works, because whereas a painting occupies space on a wall, in an altogether different way, streaming video occupies only a little memory on a server. Museums nevertheless would appear to be falling back on their familiar ways in filtering what experiences their on-site and online visitors are to have, instead of recognizing that the old models of eleven-week exhibitions in finite spaces do not have much to do with these new ways of making art.

Furthermore, the whole reason to choose among thousands of paintings for purchase and display in museums is to set a standard for appreciation, implicitly excluding those pictures that are felt to be second-tier. The museum must use limited financial resources for purchasing a finite number of works that will occupy limited gallery and storage space, be described in the limited space of analog publications, and attract a finite number of visitors. In the digital realm, however, there is no necessary limit on the number of works to be featured, displayed, published, or seen. The choices are limited instead only by the appetite and tastes of the consumer.

The extent to which the curator's palate is discerning is a huge problem. Without any practical reason to limit oneself to a finite number of works worth advocating, art historians in this new generation are in a double bind. Their Lacanian training has led them to resist categorization of works of art according to a presumed hierarchy of quality, which is also felt to be the domain of nineteenth-century colonial oppressors. Add to that the realization that there is no need to use quality as a shield from squandering limited resources, because the resources are notionally almost infinite, and conservators will be faced with the insurmountable challenge of possibly having to preserve every scrap of code made by every artist at work at a given time.

So what we must do, alas, is to introduce that tried-and-true technique for winnowing: the marketplace. Once digital artists find themselves trying to sell their work by licensing finite versions of it, the familiar and inexorable forces of greed, acquisitiveness, and aesthetic judgment will again assert themselves, and we will no longer have the same problems of scale.

On the practical front, the second problem we face is that we have much to learn from art of the last century about the physical challenges of preserving art made with digital media. Beginning with artists who used collage, assemblage, found objects, industrial multiples, and Conceptual, Process, Performance, and Anti-Form techniques, the preservation of artistic intention may be as significant as—or even more significant than—the preservation of particular manifestations of that intention. We face a losing battle in attempting to conserve various perishable ingredients of artworks that were devised to explore alternatives to traditional craftsmanship or even to sabotage it. In such cases, it is important to document the intention of the artist through a direct exchange, with a series of questions answered. These include the artist's flexibility regarding transferring analog works to digital platforms. Artists' resistance, while understandable, may consign their works to a parallel track of public appreciation, because the equipment necessary to show films and recordings will eventually demand the specialization available only within institutions. It could be that these analog works will come to resemble texts written in an unfamiliar alphabet; we know they exist, but until they are converted into an alphabet with which we are familiar, they will not occupy much of our mental bandwidth.

The artist's flexibility toward experiential platforms is never guaranteed. Will a film from the 1970s, if transferred to DVD (digital videodisc), remain a work of art in the eyes of the artist or become a documentary equivalent lacking in its fullest experiential dimensions? Will a video from the 1980s, if streamed through a Web site, lose its value as it loses the granular quality of its original presentation?

Much is being done to study how to preserve disk and tape-based memory. At present, although estimates vary, the contents of a CD-ROM (compact disc-read-only memory) are believed to be subject to corruption within ten years, and a 3.5-inch floppy disk can begin to deteriorate in eighteen months. The 1996 report of the Task Force on the Archiving of Digital Information proves that digital information, even in laboratory conditions, cannot remain stable forever.[1] Discs and tapes are perishable and, unlike their paper-based ancestors, do not give us much advance notice about the problem. Even films at least can begin to reek of vinegar to alert us that they are near their end. In a report dated January 1999, Jeff Rothenberg maintained that although we should always push forward with the most advanced hardware and software solutions, we should ensure that these new solutions do not make previous platforms obsolescent.[2] This of course flies in the face of a primary corporate strategy in a market economy, which is to force us to buy a new version of each hand-held device as often as possible.

On the third front—facing the Protean fluidity of the digital realm—we can be certain that art-making itself will change by virtue of digital media, and not simply in response to changing platforms. The individual artist may find herself or himself tempted to work in combination with other artists around the world, simply because art-making will not be isolated from other kinds of creative exercises on an instantaneous global network traveling through the air to receivers and transmitters that are hand-held, worn, or even implanted. Automatic gestures have been part of the history of art from Dada to Surrealism to Abstract Expressionism to scatter pieces. These represent, however, only early manifestations of what could become possible with countless participants free-associating through voice-recognition technology. We may face a diminished appreciation of originality as a value integral to making art and an enhanced appreciation of interactivity and participation. We may even come to disavow the "completed" artwork altogether, when a work's continuous refreshing becomes the artist's prerogative.

The conservation challenges presented by digital flexibility begin with the ease of change made possible by computer codes. When an artist paints a painting, she or he makes choices based on a strategy tied to materials. The size of a canvas, the method of building up a surface, the length of time during which paint is in a liquid state are but a few of the factors that are essentially inflexible. Once a path is chosen, the painter has fewer options than one might at first imagine. By contrast, the artist working with digital media can change his or her work at a whim and need never consider the work finished, as in the case of a Web page or a digital file. Some artists see their Web sites as iterative, ongoing works of art with no beginning and no end. And it will be up to those seeking to preserve the experiences as the artist provides them with a reasonable simulacrum of such a work as new platforms emerge.

For two decades, we have laughed off the profession of television repairman as a pre-information age relic, since all electronics are now disposable, with limited shelf lives, cheaper to replace than to repair. Suddenly we awaken from a market-induced slumber, as those fascinating junkyards of my youth, filled with the possibilities of new life breathed into dormant mechanical devices, may soon be treasure houses for museums, filled with priceless lost parts.

The disposable society we have created has changed over the last handful of years. Ersatz antiques distressed courtesy of Ralph Lauren were requisite in the 1980s. Today our disdain for the authentic but recent antique is suddenly being over-turned, as retro fashions bring back 1950s kitchen furniture only recently deemed embarrassingly passé. Just like the earli-est Sony Portapak cameras, the microprocessors that were home to the first Mosaic browser are now priceless vintage devices, and the earliest IBM personal computers stand to be reawakened after a RAM-envy induced slumber—that is, in-duced by the illusion of constantly growing capacities for storage in random-access memory, or RAM—of two decades.

Even with an ambitious effort to reanimate forgotten recording and projection equipment, we will have to make peace with the likelihood that the original character of a digital experience will never be recaptured in its entirety. Through meticulous conventional documentation by inter-viewing artists, we will have to accommodate ourselves to the emulation of experiential conditions instead of their replica-tion. The tolerance of relative degrees of accuracy on the part of artists and experts will be tested as we make our way into the uncertain waters that lie ahead.

PEOPLE, BUILDINGS, AND COLLECTIONS

COLLECTIONS

Innovations in Security and Preservation

20. Making the Library of Congress Secure · *Innovation and Collaboration*

 Kenneth E. Lopez

"How much security is too much or too little?" is a tough question, especially for managers who are charged with preserving and protecting their institution's collections. Funding constraints alone might make the question seem irrelevant, because most of us perceive that we never get enough funding. I believe, however, that the answer lies in assessing that delicate balance between access and security. As we all know, there is a natural tension between the access required by staff and patrons and the security controls installed to prevent theft and mutilation of the collections.

My brief reply to the question of how much security is too much focuses on the issue of authorized staff and user access. If security controls in place or contemplated essentially deny access, then a library or museum becomes nothing more than a secure storage vault. Yes, the collections would be secure, but denying access to authorized users also robs the institution of its essential mission.

Indicators of too little security for the collections are systematic losses and mutilation of collection materials, highlighting the need for increased controls. Many of us have faced challenges in this area, which all too often find their way into the press. So, again, institutions must continue this delicate balancing act, enabling authorized access while minimizing the risk of exposure created by vulnerabilities to the threat of theft and mutilation. A tall order and tough challenge for all of us in this business.

One helpful approach is to focus on "innovation" in collections security planning, innovation in terms of approaches to building a workable and effective security program for cultural institutions. I am not referring to "technical" innovations, as in closed-circuit television, intrusion-detection systems, electronic access controls, or key tracking capabilities. I would like instead to highlight innovations pursued at the Library of Congress in terms of building a common framework for assessing risk and the collaborative approach we have developed in sustaining our security programs. The following background items place these innovations in perspective.

Before 1997, the approach taken by the Library of Congress to security was fragmented and lacked an overall strategy. In 1997, the disparate functions were consolidated under the central control of a single entity, the Office of Security. One of the first tasks of the Office of Security was to articulate the Library's vision for security. This vision or strategy has been captured in the October 1997 Library of Congress Security Plan. The Security Plan defined the threat to the collections and focused on creating a planning framework of physical security controls to protect the Library's collections. It also established parameters for the Library to protect its facilities, staff, visitors, and other assets.

The Security Plan describes the tiers of risk categorizing our collections, their cycles, and the minimum standards adopted for physical security controls. The plan establishes an innovative framework for the Library to assess risk, identify its unmet requirements, and build budget requests to address these critical needs (see chapter 4).

Outside auditors conducting risk assessments in select custodial and processing divisions adopted the plan's framework of risk in assessing vulnerabilities and control weaknesses. These risk assessments outline a critical path of actions that each division must address to minimize its vulnerabilities to theft and mutilation.

Perhaps most important, the plan's framework has enabled the Library to integrate its security needs in comprehensive budget packages cutting across our separate curatorial and processing divisions. For the first time, the Library can summarize for its funder—the Congress—the status of needs across the Library and can project timelines for addressing these requirements. Institutions rarely gain all funding requested for security. We now, however, can depict what controls are needed to protect the collections across a commonly shared framework of risk.

No single office could have accomplished all these tasks in a vacuum. The Library of Congress adopted a wholly integrated, collaborative effort to capture the insights and needs of our principal operating units. The Office of Security collaborated with the Collections Security Oversight Committee (CSOC) to develop its plan and an implementation strategy that remains in place today. The CSOC, its four standing subcommittees, and ad hoc working groups have a continuum of initiatives that over time will create a more secure environment for the Library's collections.

Following the publication of the Security Plan in October 1997 addressing minimum standards for physical security controls for the collections, the CSOC spearheaded development of standards for preservation, bibliographic, and inventory management controls within the plan's framework of risk. To date, preservation controls have been integrated with the physical security controls described in the 1997 Security Plan (see chapter 7). Again, the common framework and language have facilitated communication between separate disciplines. The task is a work in progress, but progress indeed has been and will continue to be made.

The Library has also contracted with an outside auditor to conduct objective random sampling projects in select divisions, with the intent of establishing over time credible baselines of theft and mutilation. To date, the projects have yielded positive results, showing no theft or mutilation in one of our most heavily used special collections—a clear indicator that our security controls are working.

Beginning in April 2000, a special CSOC working group initiated a project to test the feasibility of developing minimum standards for controls to protect the Library's digitized collections. An extensive external peer review of the group's work to date is now under way. The intensity of the Library's effort to develop security controls protecting the collections has also encompassed the Library's need to protect its facilities, staff, and visitors from a wide array of threats, which range from terrorist attacks to individual acts of violence directed toward our staff. As a result of the shooting of two U.S. Capitol Police officers at the Capitol in July 1998, followed by the U.S. embassy bombings in East Africa, Congress directed significant physical security improvements for the Capitol complex, including the Library's three main buildings. The Library developed a Security Enhancement Implementation Plan in February 1999, addressing requirements articulated in the 1997 Security Plan. The physical security enhancement plan is a multiyear program of security upgrades to strengthen the Library's established minimum standards for police command and control, entry and perimeter security, and related law enforcement enhancements to conform with the overall Capitol complex security objectives.

Under the Security Enhancement Implementation Plan, the Library is building a new consolidated Police Communications Center to integrate the Library's intrusion detection and security monitoring systems. The Library is also expanding entry and perimeter security to include additional screening equipment and associated modification of building entrances, exterior monitoring cameras and lighting, and garage and parking lot safeguards. The design phase for these projects is complete, and construction and installation will take place over the next two years.

In conclusion, I would like to summarize insights we have gained at the Library of Congress over the past several years as we have developed our security program:

(1) A clear strategy for an integrated approach to protect people, buildings, and collections must be established.

(2) It is important that libraries and other cultural institutions develop a framework of risk creating a common language across their organizational units to facilitate cooperation across separate functional disciplines.

(3) Collaboration among all involved entities is essential to building an integrated approach to security.

(4) Cultural institutions must preserve the authorized access of staff and patrons while balancing the risks such access poses.

(5) There must be a commitment to invest in physical security improvements that will significantly enhance the security of our facilities, our people, and the heritage assets entrusted to us for safeguarding.

The Library has made much progress in securing and preserving its unique collections and upgrading facilities security, with the continuous support of Congress. The Library's security program is a dynamic, evolving program that ensures that the Library can sustain this progress within an established security management structure that can adapt to changing threats and new technology.

21. What Can We Afford to Lose?

 Abby Smith

Preservation is deemed an excellent thing by all, yet is funded by few. Why? What prevents institutions and individuals from being willing to "pay their way" in this area as they are willing to do so in many others: cataloging, acquisitions, hardware, and software?

There are a number of factors at work, some of which are social, some psychological, and some of which have to do with traditional library business practices.

First, we must acknowledge that there are powerful social forces that keep preservation from competing successfully for our attention. We are not a culture of ancestor worshipers here in America. On the contrary, our culture places high value on things having immediate reward, no matter how small, over against those having delayed benefits, no matter how great. The national savings rate, which is now calculated to be in negative territory, is but one exemplar of this attitude. The savings rate is below our rate of expenditures either because we choose to ignore warnings about the need to save for the future, or, for those more financially savvy, because the return on investment available on the market makes saving appear to be a waste of time and resources. The so-called new economy is booming precisely because of technologies—information technologies primarily—that maximize immediate return over long-term gains.

Something parallel is occurring in the current sociology of libraries. These same information technologies are making libraries more effective at delivering services to their patrons anytime, anywhere. One of the unintended consequences of these technologies, though, is that they divert libraries' attention from preservation to access. They divert not only our attention, but also our funds. The reasons are not hard to see. We all feel an urgent sense to keep up with the fast pace of technological change, and to do so takes enormous sums of money, involving us in a never-ending search for good people, because we cannot seem to retain our best people for long, and obliging us to educate our funding bodies and trustees about the consequences of changes that we do not ourselves fully understand.

Second, preservation has lost its sense of urgency for what might be called professional psychological reasons. With so much to do, why do today what you can put off until tomorrow? This psychological preference for instant gratification over delayed gratification is perfectly understandable. Frankly, delayed gratification too often feels like no gratification, for in the preservation game, the pay-off is indirect, accruing to others. In a way, even preservation people have to admit the intractability of this psychological disadvantage. It is generally easier to recruit bench conservators than preservation managers, because the rewards of handling the materials are so immediate. Repairing damaged items often feels better than preventing damage in the first place.

But as professionals, have we really lost the sense that we are the beneficiaries of the actions of those who came before us? I do not think so. At the end of the day, the chief stumbling block to funding preservation is that we have yet to find the right answer to the key question: "What is the value of this stuff, and what benefit as individuals, institutions, and a society do we derive from keeping and sharing it?"

We do not understand how to demonstrate the value of preservation in a meaningful way. People struggle constantly to do so and nearly always fall back on anecdotes, usually involving item-level conservation. We could, of course, put a dollar value on our collections, but that tends to fix the value of individual objects as they would be valued if they were to appear on the market today. Artifactual value may effectively be calculated this way; but what about objects that have high intrinsic research and information value but little artifactual value? In considering artifacts, take the example of the Bible that Abraham Lincoln held when he took the oath of office as president, an item found in the Library of Congress's collections and often trotted out to give potential donors and visiting potentates a case of the shivers. Frankly, its research value is close to nil. It is one of an undistinguished print run, and the text is well known, to say the least. If we lost that item, we would lose no information. But to the extent that it has associational value, it clearly is irreplaceable. Because of the charisma that attaches to it through association, that Bible would fetch a handsome price were it to go on the market. And because of its charisma, it is the beneficiary of strict security protocols and responsible preservation care.

But what about those other items in a research collection that have no appreciable market value but are, in their own way, equally irreplaceable—sheet music from the nineteenth century, for example? Or the early editions of *Huckleberry Finn*—not the first edition, but subsequent ones that yield so much information about the reading public of the time. How do we avoid the problem of having to replace items like that? The best approach for securing these institutional assets—for that is what they are—is to identify the factors that put these items at risk as objects with research value, and to mitigate those risks in the most cost-effective way possible with current technologies. This is what I refer to as the risk assessment model. It works for collections that include items of high financial value as well as high research value.

This approach does not ask the question "How much can we afford to spend on preservation?" That answer, as we all know, is "never enough." With an answer like that, it is hard to know where to begin to invest the resources we do have, no matter how inadequate. Rather, I propose that we ask "How much can we afford to lose?"—knowing full well that preservation is about reasonable trade-offs, that technology will offer us solutions in the future that we do not even dream of now, and that planning for failure is the best way to mitigate its effects.

Library preservation differs from museum preservation in that libraries are always looking to the item's use and fitness for purpose. The risk assessment model I propose here is focused entirely on fitness for purpose: how is that object going to be used? Let us take an ordinary library object—a book. What threatens a book, makes it useless? It could be misplaced, inadvertently misshelved. It could be incorrectly cataloged and hence unretrievable, or it could be languishing uncataloged in a backlog somewhere on a book truck or cataloger's desk. It could be embrittled and crumble when you turn pages. Or it could be physically damaged through vandalism—the illustrations razored out—or just plain stolen. In the language of risk assessment, these risks pertain to:

(1) inventory control: where is it?
(2) bibliographical control: what is it?
(3) preservation control: is the information intact and the item usable? and
(4) security control: is the item unduly at risk of theft or mutilation?

What is useful about this approach, in my view, is that it describes the day-to-day business of libraries, only in a language that is more accessible to financial officers, presidents, and CEOs than the terms we use among ourselves. Libraries having significant collections are increasingly directed by or responsible to men and women who are not trained librarians. As vitally interested in the health and well-being of their institutions as they are, they do not share the same assumptions, skills, and expertise as catalogers, preservation specialists, and curators. As individuals having fiduciary and financial responsibilities for the institutions they oversee and their assets, they make or are responsible for difficult choices in a time of increasing demands on essentially flat budgets. One of the advantages of a risk assessment model for library collections is that it defines those collections as primary institutional assets, an inventory built up over decades and centuries that is critical to the ability of a library to fulfill its mission: to serve its patrons the information and cultural resources they need. It defines the collections not as sunk costs, but as primary investments that need additional funds to keep them productive.

In partnership with KPMG Peat Marwick, the Library of Congress developed and has implemented a risk assessment model for the management of its collections, known in the federal accounting trade as "heritage assets"—a bewitching term—a term that I understand means that the value of this asset can never be used up. The risk assessment, conducted every year during the institutional audit, works from established benchmarks and provides a rational basis for developing long-range plans and the budgets to implement them. In other words, it is based on evidence—objectively and systematically gathered data about the state of the holdings and their vulnerability to various risks. It provides a flexible and common framework for determining the needs of collection items as various as baseball cards, videotapes, incunabla, and microforms. The value of each type of item in the collections is defined by its purpose, and the well-being of that item by its fitness for purpose, which makes this approach dynamic and focused on the use or potential use of that item.

This model is described in great detail in a report published by the Council on Library and Information Resources in cooperation with the Library of Congress, *Managing Cultural Assets from a Business Perspective*.[1] The report begins from the premise that, because these are the primary assets of the institution, the question is not "How much can we afford to pour into these collections?" but rather, "How much risk do we take if we fail to invest in our asset base?" It guides managers in identifying specific risks in their libraries and deciding what level of risk is acceptable versus unacceptable. It provides a step-by-step description of a process of risk evaluation that involves everyone in the institution who is responsible for the collections. This means not only those who work directly with collections, but also those responsible for security, buildings and grounds, and, most important, the information technology infrastructure. After all, inventory and bibliographical controls are absolutely essential to all aspects of security, preservation, and service. So, whoever maintains the Online Public Access Catalog (OPAC), the integrated library system, and keeps it up and running, is as critical to the good stewardship of library collections as a cataloger or a rare book conservator.

This model works just as well with digital assets as with rare books or the treasures in the nitrate film vaults in Ohio. With respect to digital assets, it seems clear to many thoughtful people that the growing availability of information online raises the essential question, "Do we really need all this stuff in the first place?" Are we not best off putting our scarce preservation resources into items that will be selected for an exhibition or digitized for Web distribution—something, in other words, with a probable—a calculable—demand for access? As library materials become increasingly available on the Web, do we really need to keep a lot of the nondigital resources that we have now?

The answer, of course, is that many if not most of the items research libraries acquire have been collected for their research value. Because of the numerous constraints on doing research on the Web, many of these materials will never be digitized—not just because they are intrinsically low-use, but because they are valuable chiefly in the original or may, owing to copyright issues, be used only that way.

But what is research value? This is a question given too little examination, in my view. It seems to be a lot like pornography—we cannot define it per se, but we all know it when we see it.

But of course, the problem is that we often do not know it when we see it. That is certainly the basis for Nicholson Baker's criticism of libraries' treatment of original newspapers. How many decisions have we made in the past—not only about deaccessioning and pulping, but even about rebinding—that we now regret, even if we try to avoid talking about it in public? How do we measure research value—what are its attributes? Do rarity, association, beauty—all the things that we recognize in the value of the artifact—have any meaning here? If so, how do we recognize these qualities? Can we develop objective criteria that allow us to discriminate between objects that must be selected and retained in a collection and those that need not be, or at least need not be retained in the original in all cases?

If we are to argue for the resources we need in order to keep collections fit and accessible, we must recognize that this is not a question that librarians and archivists can answer alone. It is all members of the research community, however you define that, who need to articulate the new role that collections are playing in the production of knowledge. The Council on Library and Information Resources (CLIR) has been working for a year now with the Task Force on the Artifact in Library Collections, composed of scholars, librarians, and academic officers, to investigate the meaning and role of the artifact in research collections in the context of current information and preservation technologies. Collections can be viewed as assets, not liabilities, only if they are vital for the institutional mission (which of course includes holding such objects of intrinsic cultural value as Lincoln's Inaugural Bible). Risk assessment is premised on the notion that one must keep these collections ready for anticipated use in order to be productive.

What does productivity mean in this environment? The productivity of that Bible is not in dispute: it is valuable for display and for fund-raising. But can we measure the relationship between, say, scholarly output and use of collections? This area is quite problematic, though important, and we must follow closely the changing research habits and strategies of our primary patrons.

In the meantime, we can draw some conclusions from our years of experience as custodians of heritage assets. Let us take a closer look at those fourth, fifth, tenth editions of *Huckleberry Finn*. An item that has research value is usually part of a larger whole that provides context for its interpretation. Even rare items are often made more valuable by existing within a collection of like and comparable things: an incunable is made more valuable by being part of a number of similar imprints that, through study and comparison, give the first additional value. Neither does *Huckleberry Finn* exist in the vacuum of an exhibition case. First published in 1885 and issued in hundreds of editions since, it illustrates the point that the research value of any given item or series of items is dynamic and largely unpredictable. It also demonstrates that the research value and the preservation strategy to serve that value can be dramatically affected by new technologies. There were probably few libraries that attempted to collect and preserve all or even most editions of this book, in large part because the text was well-known and easy to acquire. Few people thought that the history of the publication and dissemination of the text over time was an important topic for research. Until recently, that is.

A group of enterprising individuals at the University of Virginia with an interest in Twain's text, the history of the publication and reception of the text, the changing ways that various characters were represented in illustration—Jim, for example—and any number of other topics that devolve from this book gathered a variety of editions and made them available on their Web site. They have used this digital technology to create a virtual collection of the editions of this book that, with the right mark-up, allow new avenues of inquiry into the phenomenon of *Huckleberry Finn*. The technology not only allows better use, but it also renders redundant so many of the fragmentary collections that abound. But let us remember that no one asked questions about reader reception forty years ago. Chances are, reception theory, so fashionable now, will not be forty years hence.

I will close with one prognostication—not a particularly daring one. I believe that within twenty-five years, many if not most information resources will be created and distributed in digital form, and that, as a consequence, there will be a number of libraries that have amassed large collections of objects—books, maps, videos—that will find these collections, as information sources, inventory that is not worth saving. And yet, libraries that have amassed collections that are valuable as cultural objects, broadly construed, and not simply as information resources, will find their collections just as valuable and useful in the future as they do now, perhaps even more so. Libraries will come to have a higher profile as cultural institutions than as information depots. Therefore, our successors will judge us and the decisions that we make today on the basis of our discrimination between cultural value and informational value. We as stewards of library collections have much to learn from our colleagues in the museum community, and just as much from our colleagues in the information technology world, about how material objects and immaterial digits create and convey meaning.

22. National Research Libraries and Protection of Cultural Resources

 James F. Williams, II

The strategic stewardship of cultural resources requires at a minimum that research library deans or directors assume responsibility for the safety of employees and patrons, the physical protection of buildings and their contents and immediate surroundings, the establishment and implementation of protection programs concerning natural disasters, coordinated conservation and preservation programs, an asset protection policy, periodic audits of the library's assets and protection systems, and training programs related to the obligations and responsibilities of staff in all safety and security matters. As the head of a research library having unique information resources that represent the collective memory of human activity, the director or dean also has the responsibility to be a partner on the national level in the emerging national strategy to preserve and protect the nation's cultural resources. He or she must also implement this national strategy locally, in the home institution.

The forms of risk to a research library are myriad. The research library dean or director must successfully provide a reasonable level of stewardship and protection, while at the same time offering the most reasonable level of access to the library organization. This balance must be founded on a careful consideration of risks, based on past experience, events, and environmental factors. It demands also the corresponding use of countermeasures, which should usually be expected to offer the desired level of protection for the institution. Failing to reach balance on this primary compromise could ultimately create a series of secondary, negative compromises of necessity (out of the dean or director's control) that could affect the continuing significance of the library. Those negative compromises could relate to legal liability based on a failure to preserve and protect, a negative reputation for the library based on the perceived fears of patrons, and the ultimate compromise, that is, a sense that the library denies a freedom of access that had been previously enjoyed.

Numerous forms of risk to academic libraries have been described in detail in a set of guidelines published by the Safety and Security Committee of the Buildings and Equipment Section of the Library Administration and Management Association (LAMA), a division of the American Library Association.[1] These guidelines cover (1) adequacy of protection, (2) fire and emergency protection, (3) physical barrier and lock and key security, (4) security duties and security staff, (5) personal access and parcel control, and (6) security alarms and electronics.

In the early 1990s, the incidence of crime on campus was highlighted in the public press in a *New York Times Magazine* article that described the personal dangers that exist on many campuses.[2] During that same period, Congress became so concerned about the incidence of crime on campus that it passed the Crime Awareness and Campus Security Act in 1990, requiring campuses to report crime rates and types of offenses occurring on campus.[3] For academic libraries, P. Bean alleges that these institutions in particular have certain characteristics in common that make them particularly vulnerable to criminal activity. The foremost of these is their expectation that their assets will be taken away for use and returned at a later date.[4] Other common characteristics are open access policies, extended hours of operation, limited full-time staffing during evenings and weekends, a location on campus that may be out of the way, architectural design that creates invisible areas within the library, and a lack of security training for the staff. These characteristics lead to crimes of opportunity, whose prevalence centers on theft of collections, vandalism or mutilation, theft of personal property and library equipment, voyeurism and exhibitionism, arson, and personal assaults on staff or patrons. The bottom line is that the perpetrators of these types of crimes of opportunity probably commit their offenses because of a perception that the threat of being caught is low.

There is another major risk, however, that is not associated with crime. The inscription over the door of the main library at the University of Colorado at Boulder reads, "Who Knows Only His Own Generation Remains Always a Child" (*nescire autem quid ante quam sis acciderit, id est semper esse puerum* B Cicero, *Orator* 120). It goes without saying that the nation's research libraries continue to house and selectively preserve the record of human experience. They do so in general and special collections of unique primary resources and scholarly texts in print and many forms of other media. These collections continue to be of immense value to society and to its understanding of the past as it relates to the present and the future. Many of the invaluable items in these collections have been subjected to the vagaries of war, fire, floods, careless accidents, the wear and tear of use, and the passage of time. And others, either surrogates or those born digital, have already reached that point of extreme volatility for magnetic media that we know as physical deterioration.

Because of the highly acidic paper on which they are printed, most post-1850 print publications are at risk. In addition, as scholarship and scholarly communication become increasingly reliant on digital collections, research libraries are now faced with the complex intellectual question about which information to save—not whether to save, but what to save. The magnitude of the preservation problems in a given research library is determined by the age, scope, and composition of its various collections: collections that come in the form of monographs, journals, newspapers, maps, manuscripts, photographs, and digital images and collections that are represented on paper, vellum, film, magnetic tape, and disks of various types. Among the variety of these media, however, paper-based publications still constitute the majority of our research collections, and thus they are at the heart of the preservation crises in academic libraries. An early study at the Library of Congress, for example, found that some seventy-seven thousand of its volumes become brittle each year.[5] Risk assessment and risk management have thus become critical elements of an emerging national strategy to preserve and protect as the complex question of what collections to save is engaged both within and beyond the academy.

Although it is much easier to agree on the need for preservation than on a national strategy to preserve and protect for continued access, one key element of that emerging national strategy is to consider sharing the responsibility. The recommendation is that if a library cannot afford the full range of operational expenses associated with the successful management of special collections, it (the library) should not attempt to house and manage such collections.[6] Any national strategy to preserve and protect must be based on the defining issue of selection—selection based upon common approaches, values, and prioritization across the research library and scholarly community—as well as on the choice of format for preservation. And, if that strategy is based on sharing national responsibility to preserve and protect those cultural resources most at risk, the follow-on assumption is that the strategy must be based on the integrity of local research collections.

Integrity in the individual academy library should be defined in terms of subject or collection-based comprehensiveness and strength, integrity that must therefore be determined through a discipline-by-discipline differentiation and analysis, made by scholars and library subject specialists in each field, of what is the total literature of each field. This determination should further be based on research patterns in each field and the uniqueness of the resources in that field. With an emphasis on at-risk resources, the partners who frame the national strategy must also take into account the enduring value of some resources as artifacts.

This discipline-by-discipline selection process should not be compromised by the need for expediency. In addition, this selection process can be supplemented through secondary partnerships with learned societies, book collectors associations, antiquarian booksellers, auction houses, book dealers, and nationally known new and used bookstores. Several printed reference sources also exist through which a capability to both establish and check the current value of resources at risk may be implemented.

In the absence of such a national strategy, the members of the Association of Research Libraries (ARL) who have a preservation program currently use a variety of methods to preserve and protect their collections for future access and use. These include everything from commercial binding, to conservation treatment of rare materials, to digitization. These methods also include the storage of collections under properly controlled temperature and humidity. In 1998, the record of institutional support for preservation in ARL institutions was more than $82 million.[7] As the move to contain costs in higher education becomes a trend line, the threat to preservation programs in the research library community becomes a major challenge for scholars, librarians, and their institutions because of competition for resources. Thus, there is an immediate need to leverage existing resources through a national strategy that emphasizes collaboration and a reduction in duplicative effort while sharing the national responsibility to preserve, protect, and provide access. The blueprint for a national strategy that includes a major use of digitization for these purposes must address and solve the issues surrounding the challenge of "how to convert such collections to digital format," in Clifford Lynch's words, "in a way that facilitates reuse and enhancement by the broad scholarly community over time—that weaves primary content into a web of commentary, criticism, scholarship, and instruction, and links it to other related content without regard to institutional or geographic boundaries, while preserving the integrity of the digitized representations."[8]

With major risks associated with the preservation crises at the national level, and other risks associated with crimes of opportunity at the local level in individual research libraries, it becomes apparent that responsibility to preserve and protect is a partnership that begins at the local level. A comprehensive program of safety and security in the local research library starts at the policy level and moves from there to implementation. The development of such comprehensive policies and programs involves many offices within and beyond the institution, including facilities management, human resources, disability and access services, institutional security, risk management, the university attorneys, and law enforcement and other safety agencies in the community. At the policy level, there should be full compliance and integration of the library's policies with construction codes, with state laws related to library security, and with the regulations of the Americans with Disabilities Act, the Federal Emergency Management Association, the Occupational Safety and Health Act, and related emergency agencies. This level of compliance and integration should also assume institutional liaison and requisite reporting as related to these congressional acts and associated agencies. Compliance also assumes that the library will accept and respect the authority of the campus risk management office and police. This obligation includes attention to their analysis of risks to the library based on valuations of resources, levels and elements of liability coverage, past events, and current local, national, and international crime-watch bulletins.

The core of the library's safety and security policy must focus on adequacy of protection in all circumstances of risk. These policies should include (in no order of priority):

(1) a directory (including names and contact numbers) of those who are responsible for operations and actions during situations of risk;

(2) the rules of conduct and engagement for staff (regardless of rank) during situations of risk, in order to provide adequate protection to fellow workers and patrons, and the library's assets;

(3) specifications noting the location of the library's most valued physical assets, for instance, rare books, manuscripts, archives, and so on, for use by law enforcement and fire and other safety agencies, including a security operations review cycle specifically related to these resources and their location;

(4) specifications for the location of cold-site (versus hot-site) storage of back-ups to bibliographic and other resource-related files for reference by law enforcement and fire and other safety agencies, including a security operations review cycle specifically related to these resources and their location;

(5) a current valuation of the library's resources, highlighting those resources of highest value and at the greatest risk;

(6) an internal security plan that identifies the major threats and risks to staff, patrons, and the library's assets—a plan that anticipates each type of risk and addresses the library's specific plans (including staff training) and countermeasures for each type of threat (this internal security plan may also include a basic security operations manual for student employees or other part-time staff during those hours of operation when immediate access to upper level management is not possible);

(7) a staff training plan that includes training provided by professional safety personnel from within and beyond the institution, which, if it involves life safety assistance of fellow staff or patrons, should be approved by university attorneys as it relates to the institution's liability in certain circumstances;

(8) an emergency disaster plan that anticipates all such emergencies and includes specific staff instructions, institutional and community safety agencies that normally respond to threats of personal safety, major theft, vandalism, fire, floods, tornadoes, hazardous waste spills, and so on, and contacts for both facilities and consultants related to conservation and preservation;

(9) a comprehensive plan for special events that involve valuable assets owned by or on loan to the institution, which includes valuation of the assets involved in the event, determination of whose insurance will cover the liabilities associated with the event, the level of necessary security personnel for the event based on the valuation of assets, electronic surveillance methods, personal access and parcel control procedures, the level and nature of public relations associated with the event, donor-approval procedures related to all aspects of the event (if necessary), and pre- and post-event lock-up procedures;

(10) a statement about the institution's pre-employment screening guidelines as they relate to safety and security;

(11) a statement about the institution's qualifications for safety and security professionals, including what the staff can expect in terms of the physical, mental, and other characteristics of these professionals, once hired;

(12) where applicable, a statement about the expectations of the security employees in the library, including their jurisdiction and authority;

(13) a timetable for life safety practice sessions, evacuation drills, emergency disaster response simulations, safety equipment demonstrations, and so on, that relates to all types of threats; and

(14) a timeline for regularized security audits that review the adequacy of the following basic elements of the library's security program: (a) opening procedures, (b) closing procedures, (c) patron screening, (d) bibliographic control, (e) special collections, (f) other limited circulation collections, (g) division of labor in acquisitions operations, (h) equipment and supplies, and (i) follow-up reporting on all occurrences related to risk.

In its library security guidelines, LAMA specifies for security alarms and electronics that reliable alarm security systems require the following six characteristics:

(1) local alarm annunciation when an area is occupied;

(2) consistent and rapid human response;

(3) professional selection and application of alarm sensors for good alarm coverage;

(4) secured communication lines and back-up power supply;

(5) appropriate adjusting, testing, inspection, and maintenance; and

(6) back-up annunciation at a commercial alarm monitoring facility.[9]

The LAMA guidelines go on to describe in detail the necessity for: continuous alarm protection; interrupted alarm protection; and audible and visual alarm annunciation. They specify overlapping security protection for high-security areas, with alarms to central stations that are monitored twenty-four hours a day and consistent and rapid response to security alarm annunciation during and after library hours of operation. Magnetic contact or micro switches should be in place on exterior perimeter openings, and glass-break detecting sensors or volumetric motion detection sensors should be in place on perimeter exterior surfaces with glass, as well as combination volumetric motion detection sensors to detect unauthorized persons in the library when it is closed.

For special collections, these precautions are augmented by the placement of magnetic contact or micro switches on all openings; vibrator alarm sensors on all flat surfaces to detect forced entry from unprotected areas; and microdot tags and radio frequency field labels in high-risk materials (for libraries with exit detection systems). Closed-circuit television systems, alarm key-pads with a confidential code to authenticate persons who open and close the library, and silent duress or panic alarms for persons who open and close the library are indicated. The guidelines also recommend hard-wired or wireless alarm systems with control panels; back-up and secure annunciation systems to an outside alarm monitoring facility (or municipal police or similar emergency dispatch station) that follows UL Standard 1610 for central station alarm units and meets UL Grade AA Communication Link requirements; and, last but not least, provision for alternative power supplies or generators.[10]

Additional security modifications should also include state-of-the-art archival storage rooms and vaults for special collections. To guard against crimes of opportunity, additional technological modifications may also include (1) enhanced card key systems, (2) surveillance cameras, (3) duress alarms at service desks, (4) scream alarms in restrooms, (5) portable alarm devices for staff, (6) communications systems for full staff alerts, and (7) computer security systems to protect against abuse or malicious use. The library market has already seen the introduction of automated inventory control and access systems that operate on radio frequency field labels that are integrated with patron identification and local library systems. These radio-frequency-based systems provide automatic circulation of materials, real-time inventory control, detailed use statistics at the material and patron level, immediate location of materials that are not in circulation, and the added advantage of security control against unauthorized users.

Because digitization holds the promise as one of the best ways to reformat and preserve resources at risk while providing networked access to them, the framers of a national strategy to preserve and protect must face the reality that there is no existing standard for the archival permanence of digitized resources. In the absence of such national standards, best practices and community-based standards are being applied across the country.

These ad hoc standards are based on the work of recognized leaders in the field of digitization, such as the Council on Library and Information Resources, Cornell University, the Digital Library Federation, the Library of Congress, the Online Computer Library Center, the Research Libraries Group, and the University of California, Berkeley.[11] Most of the existing community-based standards developed to date should be viewed as minimum recommended standards with accompanying guidelines for the application of those standards. They typically contain sections on scanning, metadata creation and entry, copyright, and collection development policy and selection. Taken as a corpus of digital project resources, these community-based standards and guidelines constitute a de facto national standard for those institutions entrusted with the strategic stewardship of cultural resources.

The strategic stewardship of cultural resources is a responsibility of immense proportions for the nation's museums, archives, and research libraries. This stewardship involves the daily security and preservation of the vast historical and intellectual records of human experience—records that are the foundation of scholarship, teaching, and discovery. Because of the kind and content of the risks—both real and perceived—associated with these resources, the need for coordinated national programs to preserve and protect them is apparent. At a minimum, national stewardship responsibilities place a corresponding local responsibility on the research library dean or director for the safety of employees and patrons, buildings, and collections. Protection programs related to natural disasters, coordinated conservation and preservation programs, and an asset protection policy are all necessary. Programs to audit asset and protection systems and adequate training programs for staff in all safety and security matters are essential elements of this stewardship. Local responsibility for security and preservation also means that the research library director must anticipate risks to cultural resources and thus maintain safeguards to prevent predictable losses associated with the major forms of risk.

Best practice—based on best knowledge—dictates a primary compromise on the question of how much security is too much or too little. That compromise must provide a reasonable level of stewardship and protection, while offering the most reasonable level of access to our cultural resources. It is a compromise that should be formalized in policy and founded on an ongoing consideration of risks and the use of innovative and effective countermeasures, which would usually be expected to offer the desired level of protection for an institution and its assets.

Conclusion

 Winston Tabb and Mark Roosa

"To Preserve and Protect" brought together a wide range of participants from a variety of backgrounds. Our speakers engaged us in a number of topics, and all our participants had the opportunity to discuss areas of common concern.

As we consider where we go from here, let us review some of the themes that emerged. One of our greatest anxieties at the Library of Congress, entering into the symposium, was that the nexus between security and preservation, which seemed so natural to us at the Library, might seem like a shotgun marriage to others. But it was reassuring to see, as the symposium progressed, that more and more speakers referred to the link between protecting and preserving as if it were obvious.

From the first day of the symposium, the welcoming remarks by Librarian James Billington reminded us of the responsibility that we all share in preserving and protecting our heritage assets, pointing to the importance of collaboration and the urgent need for coordinated action both nationally and internationally to achieve this goal. Shirley Baker, vice chancellor for information technology and dean of university libraries at Washington University in St. Louis, reminded us on that day that this challenge extends to information stored in new formats and will require that we rethink the notion of artifactual value in the preservation equation. In response to a request from the General Accounting Office that the Library of Congress place a precise monetary value on its collections, the Library has taken integrated steps to provide physical security, preservation, bibliographic control, and inventory control for its collections, as we outline in chapter 4.

"Cultural Heritage at Risk: Today's Stewardship Challenge" explored some of the relationships that cultural institutions and their funders maintain and the shared and divergent expectations that each have. Werner Gundersheimer reminded us of what happens when things technological "bite back," citing 100,000 feet of microfilm in the Folger's collections that have become infected with the vinegar syndrome, advising us to maintain a "healthy skepticism" for technological innovation aimed at preserving our cultural assets. With regard to Nicholson Baker's critique of newspaper preservation, he noted that—like it or not—librarians are not alone in the business of caring for the long-term preservation of the cultural patrimony. Describing the "Janus Factor," Nancy Cline pointed to how security and preservation are fundamentally and inextricably linked to one another, as different sides of the same coin, and added that to create an environment where access and protection are in equilibrium, all parts of an organization must be on board.

With an eye toward identifying actions that cultural institutions might take to address preservation and security concerns on an institutional basis, we organized four sessions around the theme "Mobilizing for the Future: Strategies, Priorities, and Expectations for Preservation and Security."

"As Strong as Its Weakest Link: Developing Strategies for a Security Program" explored the components of institutional security programs and addressed minimum requirements for these efforts. Laurie Sowd reminded us that no matter the type of institution we work in, or what our areas of responsibility, the essential ingredients for a successful security program are people, technical systems, and policies and procedures, tied together with effective training. Steven Herman described the Library of Congress's integrated collections security plan, which aims to identify the risk status of items as they are processed, stored, used, transported, and exhibited. Charles Lowry reviewed actions the University of Maryland libraries have taken to assess their security and safety policies and procedures in partnership with the Association of Research Libraries to reinforce a philosophy of shared responsibility among all staff.

"The Big Picture: Preservation Strategies in Context" proposed models for determining preservation priorities while questioning current preservation views. Jan Merrill-Oldham posed the questions of whether digitizing is an effective replacement for microfilming as the method of choice for preserving information printed on decaying paper and whether we can realistically preserve the digital resources that we create, however carefully crafted. Doris Hamburg described the architecture of the Library of Congress's preservation security plan, integrated within its overall collections security plan. Jeffrey Field reported on the support provided by the National Endowment for the Humanities since 1979 to develop a national preservation infrastructure by strengthening the capacity of institutions to care for their collections, with the intent of preserving significant humanities collections.

"The Silver Lining: Coping with Theft, Vandalism, Deterioration, and Bad Press" examined the way bad experiences can sometimes lead to good things, including the improvement of preservation and security measures. Jean Ashton described the theft of $1.3 million worth of codices, early printed books, presidential letters, medieval documents, business papers, and maps from Columbia University in 1994 and how this affected the staff and served as a siren call for action. Lynne Chaffinch described investigations she has been involved in as manager of the Federal Bureau of Investigation's Art Theft Program, with resulting legal action taken to capture and prosecute thieves of cultural property. She discussed the dramatic theft by two men disguised as police officers who broke into the Isabella Stewart Gardner Museum in Boston, Massachusetts, on Saint Patrick's Day 1990 and stole pieces of art—including works by Rembrandt, Degas, Manet, and Vermeer—valued at approximately $300 million, which have never been recovered. Her tale reminded us of the danger of placing trust solely in our traditional modes of security. Camila Alire described one of our worst nightmares—awaking to a call that millions of gallons of water had submerged the library's collections—and walked us through the stages of recovering from such a catastrophic event.

"Building the Budget: To Successfully Promote Your Program and to Meet Major Funding Demands for Preservation and Security" looked at how institutions set funding levels for preservation and security and sustain support in the face of budget uncertainty. Noting the dichotomy inherent in protecting and sharing, Nancy Gwinn encouraged us to "use the power of the original" and to build on "the strength of our past" as recipes to garner support for preservation funding. James Neal reviewed core preservation program designs and described how their elements might be target marketed to funders. He enlightened us as to some of the traditional and entrepreneurial strategies for fund-raising, reminding us to leverage our assets to generate new income streams for conservation and preservation. Deanna Marcum described the role of the Council on Library and Information Resources on the national front and asked what role preservation programs should play in the digital age. She noted that in the face of imperiled funding for preservation, the need increases for individual institutions to contribute to the national collection of scholarly resources and accept responsibility for preserving their share of materials that have lasting scholarly value.

"Understanding Success: Measuring Effectiveness of Preservation and Security Programs" supplied us with a few examples of how we might measure the impact of our preservation and security efforts. For example, James Reilly offered a new way of quantifying the impact of the storage environment on collections longevity as a basis on which to estimate the return on investment for expensive heating, ventilating, and air-conditioning costs. Francis Ponti introduced us to statistical sampling methods and identified sampling projects undertaken at the Library of Congress. In wrapping up the symposium session, Nancy Davenport, the Library of Congress's director for acquisitions, suggested that seas of statistical data could be mined to provide useful snapshots of what is going on in our collections and reminded us to ask in so doing only those questions that have quantifiable answers.

"Electronic Information and Digitization: Preservation and Security Challenges" shifted our concerns to the rapidly proliferating world of digital information and the challenges of preserving both born-digital information and format-based digital resources. Carl Fleischhauer pointed to the changing shape of preservation in the digital future and noted that although preservation of content in digital form often begins with security issues, such reasons alone are not sufficient to justify preservation of digital content. Musing on how digitization might be accomplished within an institutional context, he added that simple copying is not enough—we must also consider the migration of content, emulation of the technical environment, and digital paleography. Maxwell Anderson pointed to our instinctive devotion to preserving all artworks and intellectual property at any cost, the instability and impermanence of digital platforms, and the fluid and seemingly infinite permutations of any digital experience as the three most vexing obstacles that cultural institutions face in the digital age. Clifford Lynch brought to our attention rough spots on the digital highway, especially with regard to digital copyright issues. He noted that whereas the scholarly and publishing communities have made considerable progress preserving information in digital form—because of the commitment to permanent access shared throughout the entire community of authors, publishers, libraries, and readers involved with financing, producing, distributing, managing, and using this literature—the consumer marketplace lacks a similar shared vision, so that we face a looming copyright crisis as consumer goods move into digital form.

"People, Buildings, and Collections: Innovations in Security and Preservation" posed such questions as, "How much security or preservation is too little or too much?" "How do cultural organizations that are typically open to the public maintain appropriate security and preservation measures?" and "What are some of the innovative and effective ways that organizations have maintained this balance?" With regard to the second question, Kenneth Lopez described efforts by the Library of Congress to work across administrative divisions to protect people, buildings, and collections. On the question of how much security is enough, James Williams pointed out that our best practices must provide for a reasonable level of stewardship and protection, while also offering the most reasonable level of access to our nation's cultural resources, an effort that must be formalized in policy, founded on considerations of risk, and implemented to produce the desired level of protection for an institution and its cultural assets. Abby Smith illustrated some of the difficult choices that institutions and individuals must make when taking action to preserve cultural assets even though confronted with overwhelming amounts of information and limited preservation solutions.

She encouraged us not to be diverted from the business of preservation by the allure of new access technologies, and she challenged us to view the value of collections in relation to institutional goals and constituent needs and to examine how that value changes over time. New technologies, she points out, for creating, disseminating, and preserving information are changing our sense of the intrinsic value of library collections.

Discussion on the theme "Envisioning New Directions: Cooperation in Preserving and Securing Collections Nationally and Internationally" gave us an opportunity to respond to some of the ideas put forward with an eye toward articulating the most pressing issues we face and ways in which we might collaborate to address these concerns.

Several strong themes emerged from our discussions, as a first step toward understanding where we need to go from here to create partnerships to advance integrated preservation and security efforts in our institutions. It was intentional that we focused discussion from the final session on the notion of cooperation, with the understanding that partnerships between preservation and security programs within institutions are just taking shape and that building opportunities for future cooperation is an essential ingredient for constructing a strong infrastructure to protect cultural assets in all types of institutions.

We asked the facilitators of our breakout sessions to gather participants' ideas regarding two questions: (1) What are the top three challenges that we face in building stronger preservation and security programs? and (2) What are the top three suggestions that will help us better collaborate to strengthen our collective preservation and security capabilities? We identified some of the top challenges as the following.

- Institutions must find funding for both preservation and security.

- The impact of evolving technologies on preservation must be understood.

- It is important for us to cooperate on several levels—both within and among institutions—in our national and regional programs for preservation and security.

- Prioritization is crucial in selecting levels of importance and understanding current and potential use. It is especially important in the more complex digital world.

- We need to market preservation and security—to give them greater visibility, both internally, among stakeholders, and externally, within our communities.

- Because we lack economic models for collaboration among institutions, we should seek the help of experts in structuring models and determining how best to use them.

- We need to act as advocates within our institutions for preservation and security measures.

- We need consensus on standards for preservation of digital copies and standards for access to them.

- Our buildings must become good repositories for valuable collections through new construction or through retrofitting them to upgrade them. Facilities must meet minimum standards for preservation, security, theft suppression, and detection.

- As we shape integrated security and preservation programs and integrate them into our institutions, we should ask who the professionals are who will make this happen. What about their training, education, expertise?

This list is not exhaustive, but it does provide a start toward mapping the areas we need to focus on in the future.

After considering common challenges, we turned to developing collaborative initiatives. In the area of collections security, we shared many interesting points and examples. In particular, we seem to agree that there is a need for rigor and business-like approaches—realizing that library directors, library staff members, and scholars are all quite capable of being threats to the security of our collections and that we need to build safeguards and controls that assume the worst in human nature. As for collaborative action in this arena, the most important is rapid and open sharing of information—both about particular threats and losses as well as about techniques that we have found effective in our local settings.

In the area of preservation, three themes emerged. First, preservation must take many forms. Second, we need to pay more attention as a community to retention of the artifact. And, third, whatever we do, we must do it together, preferably as part of a coherent national strategy.

At the Library of Congress, we have made a special effort in the last decade to develop a well-rounded preservation program—to look at environmental controls, rehousing, reformatting, deacidification, digitization, and conservation as indispensable arrows in our preservation quiver, to be selected for the appropriate targets. It was encouraging to see each of these aspects of preservation assume importance at one point or another in our discussions—and no one of them ever put forward as a panacea in and of itself. We obviously have come to recognize the complexity of our task.

In regard to concern about retention of the artifact, we elicited various ideas about how important this is, how many copies of any item are needed, what kinds of formats are needed, and who should retain them. The importance of retaining the artifact surfaced among us as an issue in a sustained way that would not have typified such a conference five or six years ago.

And, finally, symposium participants developed a host of ideas about ways to promote collaboration.

It was agreed that institutions should work collaboratively to develop a greater range of tools to assess a wide variety of security and preservation needs. More conferences like "To Preserve and Protect" might identify common interests and help the preservation and security communities organize to develop a structure that makes collaboration possible. Security should be an issue added to consortia agendas. Pooling technology research and development would help us find preservation solutions. Beyond that, lobbying to clarify or modify the copyright law would help ensure our ability to preserve content. Licensed rather than owned content provisions could facilitate preservation of born-digital products. Other suggestions for collaboration included developing a shared database of potential preservation collections, building facilities that could be used by more than one institution, and developing a compelling story that could be told to convey these concerns. It is important to undertake standards development in all areas of security and preservation and to establish mechanisms for sharing information regarding security issues and infractions. We need to collaborate to preserve material by discipline or topic, identifying which institutions can tackle specific problems, selectively distributing assignments, and meeting regularly to share ideas and resources.

The Library of Congress is aware that the kind of national strategy we need must be developed thoughtfully with our major stakeholders. Many of those stakeholders were well represented in discussions at the symposium; but others, such as intellectual property owners, were not.

In any case, at the same time that the Library of Congress is committed to leadership—doing what a national library should among its community of libraries—it is also committed to leadership through collaboration. And so we would propose to advance the ideas brought forward here as a partner with the Association of Research Libraries (ARL) and the

Council on Library and Information Resources (CLIR) in the recently proposed "Joint Study on the State of Preservation Programs in American Libraries."

Some of the components such a study needs to consider if it is to lead to a coherent, compelling national preservation strategy include deacidification, last-copy responsibilities, digitization, databases with easily accessible preservation information, and environmentally safe repositories. In addition, the Library of Congress will address other issues in the near term. One such issue is copyright legalities that have hampered our progress in coping with digital materials. In addition to accelerating development of a full-production electronic copyright deposit system—which we are now working on in response to the National Academy of Sciences study *LC 21: A Digital Strategy for the Library of Congress* (July 2000)—the Library has plans to ask Congress to amend the copyright law to make clear the Library's authority to copy open-access Web material, much as the current copyright law gives the Library the authority to tape news broadcasts without infringing the network's copyrights. But more important, the Library is interested in obtaining authority to have authorized agents do this work on our behalf, under clearly delineated conditions, both for access and for preservation. Although the initial focus would be on clarifying our relationship with the Internet Archive, our current partner, this concept of "agents" could, if judiciously applied, provide an opening for forms of collaboration in collections-building and preservation beyond what we have ever dreamed of as a community.

The Library of Congress also plans to participate in a potential national collaborative initiative concerning the development of scholarly portals, described in the work that Jerry Campbell and others have done for ARL. This concept became a theme of the Library's symposium "National Libraries of the World," held on October 23–26, 2000, as well, when our new colleague from the British Library, Lynne Brindley, described an initiative in Great Britain whereby the national library and various university libraries have agreed to take on responsibility for portals in specific subject areas.

Because we often have more success with funders—certainly at the national level—when we can demonstrate that we are solving multiple national problems simultaneously, it has occurred to us that we might think for the longer term about a similar but more expansive model in the United States. Could we choose a few subjects or disciplines, divide them among several libraries, and assign each library responsibility for permanent retention of the appropriate artifacts—properly deacidified and permanently stored at fifty degrees Fahrenheit and 35 percent relative humidity; documented in an internationally accessible database; and, to the extent copyright or licenses permit, made accessible through the Internet for wide use? In this model, no library would have to give up anything, but through it we might have information and predictable behaviors on which to base acquisitions, retention, and preservation decisions that we do not now have. Such a scheme is not without problems, of course, but it is also a wonderful opportunity to realize such a concerted national preservation and access program. Let us try to make something as challenging as this happen in our lifetimes.

NOTES

1. Stewardship: The Janus Factor
Nancy M. Cline

1. Miles Harvey, *The Island of Lost Maps: A True Story of Cartographic Crime* (New York: Random House, 2000), 23.

2. Ibid., 83.

3. Ibid., 113.

4. Abby Smith, *The Future of the Past: Preservation in American Research Libraries* (Washington: Council on Library and Information Resources, 1999), 15.

5. "The Cultural Value of Books: *United States of America v. Daniel Spiegelman, Defendant*," *Gazette of the Grolier Club*, n.s. 50, 1999, 9–25.

6. Susan Allen, "Preventing Theft in Academic Libraries and Special Collections," *Library and Archival Security* 14 (1997): 40.

2. Learning to Blush:
Librarians and the Embarrassment of Experience
Werner Gundersheimer

Karen Gundersheimer, Richard Kuhta, and A. E. B. Coldiron made many helpful suggestions in the preparation of this chapter.

1. Nicholson Baker, "Deadline: The Author's Desperate Bid to Save America's Past," *The New Yorker*, July 14, 2000, 42–61.

2. For a convenient selection of Tanselle's writings on this topic, see his *Literature and Artifacts* (Charlottesville: The Bibliographical Society of the University of Virginia, 1998), especially section 2, which includes three articles: "Reproductions and Scholarship" (1989); "The Latest Forms of Book-Burning" (1993); and "The Future of Primary Records" (1996).

3. Edward Tenner, *When Things Bite Back: Technology and the Revenge of Unintended Consequences* (New York: Knopf, 1996).

4. Jutta Reed-Scott, *Preserving Research Collections: A Collaboration between Librarians and Scholars* (Association of Research Libraries, Modern Language Association, and American Historical Association, on behalf of the Task Force on the Preservation of the Artifact, 1999). On the increasing importance of special collections in the research library environment, see also Werner Gundersheimer, "Against the Grain," *RBM: A Journal of Rare Books, Manuscripts, and Cultural Heritage* 1, no.1 (2000): 14–26.

3. As Strong as Its Weakest Link: The Human Element
Laurie Sowd

This chapter incorporates information developed by Wilbur Faulk, senior project manager for the Getty Conservation Institute. Many of his ideas for training security officers appear throughout this chapter and were developed for a session the Huntingon presented at an American Association of Museums annual conference entitled "If You Don't Feed the Staff, They'll Eat the Visitor."

4. Developing a Plan for Collections Security: The Library of Congress Experience
Steven J. Herman

1. The grids are presented on the Library of Congress Web site. They show a protection prioritization matrix of physical security controls for the five tiers of risk and the five life cycles that collection items go through at the Library. Definitions for the physical security controls are included, but dots within the matrix are omitted. See <lcweb.loc.gov/bicentennial/symposia_preserve>.

5. Creating a Culture of Security in the University of Maryland Libraries
Charles B. Lowry

Lori A. Goetsch, director of public services at the University of Maryland libraries, made a significant contribution to the preparation of this chapter.

6. Building a National Preservation Program: National Endowment for the Humanities Support for Preservation
Jeffrey M. Field

1. Margaret Child, "Programs, Priorities, and Funding," in *Preservation Issues and Planning,* ed. Paul N. Banks and Roberta Pilette (Chicago and London: American Library Association, 2000), 63–81.

2. Gordon Williams, *The Preservation of Deteriorating Books: An Examina-*

tion of the Problem with Recommendations for a Solution, report of the ARL Committee on the Preservation of Research Library Materials: September 1964 (Washington: Association of Research Libraries, 1964).

3. Nancy Gwinn, "CLR and Preservation," *College & Research Libraries,* March 1981, 104–26.

4. Warren J. Haas, *Preparation of Detailed Specifications for a National System for the Preservation of Library Materials: Final Report* (Washington: Association of Research Libraries, 1972).

5. National Endowment for the Humanities, Office of Preservation, *Preservation Programs Guidelines and Application Instructions* (Washington, 1986).

6. George F. Farr, Jr., "NEH's Program for the Preservation of Brittle Books," in *Advances in Preservation and Access* (Westport, Conn.: Meckler: 1992).

7. National Endowment for the Humanities, Chairman Lynne V. Cheney to the Honorable Sidney R. Yates, April 19, 1988.

8. Sophia K. Jordan, "A Review of the Preservation Literature, 1993–1998: The Coming of Age," *Library Resources & Technical Services,* January 2000, 4–22.

9. Janet Gertz, "Selection for Preservation in the Digital Age: An Overview," *Library Resources & Technical Services,* April 2000, 97–104.

10. Abby Smith, *The Future of the Past: Preservation in American Research Libraries* (Washington: Council on Library and Information Resources, 1999). Accessed September 27, 2000, at <www.clir.org/pubs/reports/pub82/pub82text>.

7. Safeguarding Heritage Assets: The Library of Congress Planning Framework for Preservation
Doris A. Hamburg

1. The Preservation Heritage Assets Working Group (PHAWG) developed the framework from December 1998 to July 1999. PHAWG members consisted of Doris A. Hamburg, head, Preventive Conservation, Preservation Directorate (PHAWG chair); Steven J. Herman, chief, Collections Management Division, Library Services; Debra McKern, chief, Binding and Collections Care Division, Preservation Directorate; James Schenkel, protective services officer, Office of Security; and Irene Schubert, chief, Preservation Reformatting Division, Preservation Directorate.

2. The grids can be found on the Library of Congress Web site at <lcweb.loc.gov/bicentennial/symposia_preserve>. They show a protection prioritization matrix of preservation controls for the five tiers of risk and the five life cycles that collection items go through at the Library. Definitions for the preservation controls are included.

9. *Picking Up the Pieces: The Lengthy Saga of a Library Theft*
Jean W. Ashton

1. As this chapter explains, determining exactly how much time the thief has spent or will spend in jail is complicated. Our understanding was that Daniel Spiegelman was to be released in April 2001, nearly six years after the initial arrest.

2. *United States of America v. Daniel Spiegelman, Defendant.* 97 Crim.309 (LAK), United States District Court for the Southern District of New York, April 24, 1998.

3. Stephen Blumberg, convicted in 1990 of interstate transportation and possession of nineteen tons of rare books and manuscripts valued at $20 million, was sentenced to seventy-one months' imprisonment and thirty-six months' parole.

4. Diane Johnson, *Le Mariage* (New York: Dutton, 2000).

5. Miles Harvey's book is *The Island of Lost Maps: A True Story of Cartographic Crime* (New York: Random House, 2000).

6. A condensed version of Judge Kaplan's opinion was published as "The Cultural Value of Books: *United States of America v. Daniel Spiegelman, Defendant,*" *Gazette of the Grolier Club,* n.s. 50 (1999): 9–25. See also Jean Ashton, "What Is History Worth?" *Biblio,* 3:10 (1998): 26–29, and regular press coverage in the *New York Times,* 1994–99. Judge Preska's resentencing occurred on May 24, 2000, in the United States District Court for the Southern District of New York.

11. *The Silver Lining: Recovering from the Shambles of a Disaster*
Camila A. Alire

1. Halcy Enssle and Cathy Tweedie, "Why Can't Facilities Fix This?" in *Library Disaster Planning and Recovery Handbook,* ed. Camila A. Alire (New York: Neal-Schuman, 2000), 92.

2. Jim Wexler, "Using Broadcast Television to Control a Crisis," *Communication World* 10 (November 1993), 30.

3. David Zerman, "Crisis Communication: Managing the Mass Media," *Information Management* 3 (1995): 25–28.

4. Julie Wessling, e-mail to author, September 6, 2000.

5. Patricia Smith, e-mail to author, September 6, 2000.

6. Wessling, op. cit.

7. Smith, op. cit.

8. Nora Copeland, e-mail to author, September 7, 2000.

12. Funding for Preservation: The Strengths of Our Past
Nancy E. Gwinn

1. Elizabeth McCracken, *The Giant's House: A Romance* (New York: Avon, 1996), 45.

2. Charles Coleman Sellers, *Mr. Peale's Museum: Charles Willson Peale and the First Popular Museum of Natural Science and Art* (New York: W. W. Norton, 1980), 291.

13. Securing Preservation Funds: National and Institutional Requirements
Deanna B. Marcum

1. Jutta Reed-Scott, *Preserving Research Collections: A Collaboration between Librarians and Scholars* (Association of Research Libraries, Modern Language Association, and American Historical Association, on behalf of the Task Force on the Preservation of the Artifact, 1999), 13. Data from Julia Blixrud, "Preservation Expenditures Level: Microfilming, Staffing Decline," *ARL: A Bimonthly Newsletter of Research Library Issues and Actions,* no. 201 (December 1998): 14.

2. Martha Kyrillidou, Michael O'Connor, and Julia C. Blixrud, *ARL Preservation Statistics 1996–97* (Washington: Association of Research Libraries, 1998), 6.

3. Ibid., 6.

4. Data provided by the National Endowment for the Humanities to the Council on Library and Information Resources, September 29, 2000.

5. Martha Kyrillidou, *Trends in ARL Statistics, 1998–99* (Washington: Association of Research Libraries, April 10, 2000). Available through <www.arl.org>.

6. Margaret Hedstrom and Sheon Montgomery, *Digital Preservation Needs and Requirements in RLG Member Institutions* (Research Libraries Group, December 1998). Available only electronically at <www.rlg.org>.

7. Jan Merrill-Oldham, Carolyn Clark Morrow, and Mark Roosa, *Preservation Program Models: A Study Project and Report* (Washington: Association of Research Libraries, 1991).

14. Strategies for Funding Preservation and Security
James G. Neal

1. Judith Panitch, "Special Collections in ARL Libraries," report for American Research Libraries, Research Collections Committee (Washington: Association of Research Libraries, 2001).

16. Measuring Environmental Quality in Preservation
James M. Reilly

1. The author suggests, for further reading, the following publications: J. M. Reilly, D. W. Nishimura, and E. Zinn, *New Tools for Preservation: Assessing Long-Term Environmental Effects on Library and Archives Collections* (Washington: Commission on Preservation and Access, 1995), and Donald K. Sebera, *Isoperms: An Environmental Management Tool* (Washington: Commission on Preservation and Access, 1994).

17. Preservation, Security, and Digital Content
Carl Fleischhauer

1. American Memory is a set of online collections that reproduce historical materials from the collections of the Library of Congress and other participating institutions. The URL is <memory.loc.gov>.

2. The Octavo's Web site describes the company's service and lists its CD-ROM publications: <www.octavo.com>.

3. Fred B. Schneider, ed., National Research Council, Committee on Information Systems Trustworthiness, *Trust in Cyberspace* (Washington: National Academy Press, 1999).

4. Abby Smith, ed., *Authenticity in a Digital Environment* (Washington: Council on Library and Information Resources, 2000).

5. Clifford Lynch, "Authenticity and Integrity in the Digital Environment: An Exploratory Analysis of the Central Role of Trust," in Abby Smith, ed., *Authenticity in a Digital Environment* (Washington: Council on Library and Information Resources, 2000).

6. Peter B. Hirtle, "Digital Paleography" (editorial), *D-Lib Magazine* 6:4, April 2000 at <www.dlib.org/dlib/april00/04editorial>.

18. The Coming Crisis in Preserving Our Digital Cultural Heritage
Clifford A. Lynch

Amy Friedlander made many helpful suggestions in the preparation of this chapter.

19. Electronic Information and Digitization: Preservation and Security Challenges
Maxwell L. Anderson

1. Task Force on the Archiving of Digital Information, Commission on Preservation and Access and Research Libraries Group, 1996.

2. Jeff Rothenberg, *Avoiding Technological Quicksand: Finding a Viable Technical Foundation for Digital Preservation* (Washington: Council on Library and Information Resources, 1999).

21. *What Can We Afford to Lose?*
Abby Smith

1. Laura Price and Abby Smith, *Managing Cultural Assets from a Business Perspective* (Washington: Council on Library and Information Resources, March 2000), available at <www.clir.org/pubs/reports/pub90/contents>.

22. *National Research Libraries and Protection of Cultural Resources*
James F. Williams, II

1. American Library Association, Library Administration and Management Association, Buildings and Equipment Section, Safety and Security Committee, *Library Security Guidelines* (1999) available at <www.ala.org/lama/committees/bes/sslbguidelines>.

2. Anne Mathews, "The Campus Crime Wave," *New York Times Magazine,* March 7, 1993, 38.

3. "Social Science and the Citizen," *Society* 31 (March–April 1994), 2.

4. P. Bean, "An Overview of Crime in Libraries and Information Services," in M. Chany and A. F. MacDougall, ed., *Security and Crime Prevention in Libraries* (Aldershot, United Kingdom: Ashgate, 1992), 13–31.

5. Council on Library Resources, *Brittle Books: Reports of the Committee on Preservation and Access* (Washington, 1986), 8.

6. Mark Y. Herring, "Archival Treasures: Blessing—or Burden in Disguise?" *American Libraries,* August 2000, 41–43.

7. Association of Research Libraries, *ARL Preservation Statistics, 1998–99* (Washington, 2000), 15.

8. Clifford A. Lynch, "The Role of Digitization in Building Electronic Collections: Economic and Programmatic Choices," in *Selecting Library and Archives Collections for Digital Reformatting,* Proceedings from an RLG symposium held November 5–6, 1995, Washington, D.C. (Mountain View, Calif.: Research Libraries Group, 1996), 7.

9. American Library Association, Library Administration and Management Association, *Library Security Guidelines.*

10. Ibid.

11. One of the most highly recommended guides in the field has been recently published by the Research Libraries Group, the Digital Library Federation, and the Council on Library and Information Resources. Entitled *Guides to Quality in Visual Resource Imaging,* it is "designed to serve the growing community of museums, archives, and research libraries turning to imaging as a way to provide greater access to their visual resources while simultaneously preserving the original materials." The contents include: (1) Planning an Imaging Project, (2) Selecting a Scanner, (3) Imaging Systems: The Range of Factors Affecting Image Quality, (4) Measuring Quality of Masters, and (5) File Formats for Digital Masters. *Guides to Quality* is available at <www.rlg.org/visguides>.

CONTRIBUTORS

Camila A. Alire

Dean of libraries at Colorado State University in Fort Collins, Colorado, at the time of the symposium, Camila A. Alire edited the volume *Library Disaster Planning and Recovery Handbook* (New York : Neal-Schuman, 2000). She and her colleague Orlando Archibeque have presented workshops throughout the United States on library services to the Latino community. They are coauthors of *Serving Latino Communities* (New York: Neal-Schuman, 1998). Dr. Alire's research focuses on library services, specifically, those for Latinos and other minorities. An active member of numerous professional associations, Dr. Alire is the recipient of a number of honors, including being named by *Hispanic Business Magazine* as one of the 100 most influential Hispanics in the United States.

Maxwell L. Anderson

Maxwell L. Anderson is director of the Whitney Museum of American Art in New York City. He is a trustee of the American Federation of Arts and president of the Association of Art Museum Directors. He was decorated as a Commendatore by the Republic of Italy in 1990 and was named a cultural laureate of the New York City Historic Landmarks Preservation Center in 1999. Dr. Anderson's commitment to collaboration among museums has led him to work for changes in federal legislation to ensure tax equity for artists and for changes in international conventions and treaties to permit the free circulation of artworks internationally. Dr. Anderson was founding chairman of the Art Museum Image Consortium (AMICO) and director of the Art Museum Network, organizations that have established databases of museum offerings for use around the world.

Jean W. Ashton

Jean W. Ashton is director of the Rare Book and Manuscript Library of Columbia University. She began her work experience in the field of rare books in 1984, when she joined the staff at the New-York Historical Society, becoming the director of its library from 1990 to 1993. Dr. Ashton has taught at Fisk University, Hunter College School of General Studies, and Long Island University. Among her publications are *Harriet Beecher Stowe: A Reference Guide* (Boston: G. K. Hall, 1977) and, written with Iola Haverstick, Caroline Schimmel, and Mary Schlosser, *Emerging Voices: American Women Writers, 1660–1920,* a catalog for an exhibition at the Grolier Club, March 11 to May 2, 1998. She has published articles about Henry James, P. T. Barnum, early American printing, and library theft.

Lynne Chaffinch

Lynne Chaffinch, program manager for the Art Theft Program of the Federal Bureau of Investigation, manages the National Stolen Art File and provides support for agents investigating art theft cases. She has held positions in the Autry Museum of Western Heritage in Los Angeles, California, and Monticello, in Charlottesville, Virginia. Ms. Chaffinch is a member of the American Association of Museums and the International Council of Museums. She has conducted training and made presentations on the topic of art theft for national and international audiences.

Nancy M. Cline

Nancy M. Cline is the Roy E. Larsen Librarian of Harvard College. Appointed to the position in 1996, Ms. Cline is responsible for the leadership of eleven major libraries and sixty-seven departmental libraries in the Faculty of Arts and Sciences, with combined collections totaling approximately ten million items. She was founding chair and is a member of the steering committee of Harvard's Library Digital Initiative and is chair of the planning committee of the Widener Renovation Project. Ms. Cline has published and lectured widely, with a particular focus on strategic planning and other management issues, quality improvement, research libraries and computing, and telecommunications and is an active participant in national and international dialogues regarding research libraries.

Jeffrey M. Field

Jeffrey M. Field is deputy director of the Division of Preservation and Access at the National Endowment for the Humanities. He joined the Endowment's staff in 1974 and has fostered the development of humanities programs in public libraries, administered grants for preserving and providing access to collections of research resources, and administered the Endowment's U.S. Newspaper Program. Mr. Field became assistant director for the newly formed Office of Preservation in 1985, its deputy director in 1989, and deputy director of the Division of Preservation and Access in 1995. Mr. Field serves as a liaison to the National Science Foundation for the Digital Library Initiative—Phase II.

Carl Fleischhauer

Carl Fleischhauer works on the collection-digitizing effort at the Library of Congress in the National Digital Library Program. From 1990 to 1994, he coordinated the American Memory program, a pilot project that modeled the dissemination of historical collections in electronic form and, from 1994 to 1998, guided the continued production of digital collections for that program. In 1998, Mr. Fleischhauer began to coordinate a special effort to plan new approaches for the preservation of sound and video recordings. His publications include the compact disc *The Hammons Family* (1973; Cambridge, Mass.: Rounder Records, 2001), the videodisc *The Ninety-Six: A Cattle Ranch in Northern Nevada* (United States: American Folklife Center, 1986), and the photographic books *Documenting America, 1935–43,* coedited with Beverly Brannan (Berkeley: University of California Press in association with the Library of Congress, 1988), and *Bluegrass Odyssey,* written with Neil V. Rosenberg (Champaign: University of Illinois Press, 2001).

Werner Gundersheimer

Werner Gundersheimer is director emeritus of the Folger Shakespeare Library in Washington, D.C., and visiting professor of history at Williams College. His major field is Europe from 1300 to 1600, with special emphasis on Italian and French intellectual, social, and urban history. Dr. Gundersheimer lectures widely, serves on numerous boards, and is a consultant to various scholarly organizations. A past president of the National Humanities Alliance, he is the author of several books, including *Ferrara: The Style of a Renaissance Despotism* (Princeton, N.J.: Princeton University Press, 1973), as well as many articles and reviews. He is a member of the American Philosophical Society and holds four honorary degrees.

Nancy E. Gwinn

Nancy E. Gwinn is director of the Smithsonian Institution Libraries, a twenty-two-branch system with facilities in Washington, D.C., Edgewater, Md., New York City, and the Republic of Panama. Before joining the Smithsonian in 1984, Dr. Gwinn served at the Research Libraries Group and Council on Library Resources, gaining extensive experience in the field of preservation as a manager, consultant, and author. Among her publications is *Preservation Microfilming: A Guide for Librarians and Archivists* (Chicago: American Library Association, 1987), which was awarded the Waldo Gifford Leland Prize of the Society of American Archivists in 1988. She is currently American Library Association representative to the International Federation of Library Associations Standing Committee on Preservation and chairman of the Association of Research Libraries Committee on Preservation of Research Library Materials.

Doris A. Hamburg

Doris A. Hamburg, at the time of the symposium head of Preventive Conservation at the Library of Congress, is currently director of preservation programs at the National Archives and Records Administration. A former head of Paper Conservation at the Library, in that position she oversaw all conservation work on the Library's rare collections of art, manuscripts, photographs, maps, and other unbound materials on paper. She led the effort to develop and undertake the preservation/security assessment program at the Library. From this effort came the comprehensive preservation security program used at the Library in its overall collections security program. Ms. Hamburg has served as a consultant in preservation to institutions and individual collections throughout the world.

Steven J. Herman

Steven J. Herman has been chief of the Collections Management Division at the Library of Congress since the division was established in 1978. In this position, he manages the Library's general collections, which consist of twelve million books and bound periodicals, as well as other collections assigned to the division. Mr. Herman has played a key role in the security of the collections and in particular in the development of the collections security program beginning in 1992. He was a key member developing the Library's integrated security plan for the collections, and he continues to collaborate on planning and implementing the various actions in the collections security program.

Kenneth E. Lopez

Kenneth E. Lopez was appointed as the Library of Congress's first director of security in February 1997, when all security programs of the Library were consolidated under a newly established Office of Security. Mr. Lopez has managerial responsibility for the Library's protective services, police force, personnel security, and criminal investigation functions. In addition, Mr. Lopez is chairman of the Library's Collections Security Oversight Committee. Before coming to the Library of Congress, Mr. Lopez headed federal agency security programs at the Department of Justice, Department of State, National Aeronautics and Space Administration's John F. Kennedy Space Center, and Federal Aviation Administration.

Charles B. Lowry

Charles B. Lowry is dean of libraries at the University of Maryland in College Park, where he has been the principal investigator on federal grants and foundation grants and has served as a consultant on library building projects, technology, organization, and management. Dr. Lowry has published articles and commentary on library management and organization, information technology, and cooperation. He is the founding executive editor of a new journal from the Johns Hopkins Press, *Portal: Libraries and the Academy,* and is past editor of the American Library Association's *Library Administration and Management.*

Clifford A. Lynch

Clifford A. Lynch has been director of the Coalition for Networked Information (CNI) since 1997. The coalition, jointly sponsored by the Association of Research Libraries and Educause, includes about two hundred member organizations concerned with the use of information technology and networked information to enhance scholarship and intellectual productivity. Before joining CNI, Dr. Lynch spent eighteen years at the University of California, for the last ten as director of library automation. He is past president of the American Society for Information Science and a fellow of the American Association for the Advancement of Science. Dr. Lynch currently serves on the Internet 2 Applications Council, the National Research Council Committee on Broadband Last-Mile Technology, and the National Digital Preservation Strategy Advisory Board of the Library of Congress.

Deanna B. Marcum

Deanna B. Marcum is president of the Council on Library and Information Resources (CLIR). The council's mission is to identify the critical issues that affect the welfare and prospects of libraries and archives and the constituencies they serve, convene individuals and organizations in the best position to engage these issues and respond to them, and encourage institutions to work collaboratively to achieve and manage change. Dr. Marcum has had a varied career, including serving as director of Public Service and Collection Management at the Library of Congress and dean of the School of Library and Information Science at the Catholic University of America in Washington, D.C.

Jan Merrill-Oldham

Jan Merrill-Oldham, Malloy-Rabinowitz Preservation Librarian, directs the work of the Weissman Preservation Center in the Harvard University Library and the Preservation and Imaging Department in the Harvard College Library. Together these programs provide a broad range of services to the libraries at Harvard, including special and general collections conservation, microfilming, digitizing, studio photography, photoduplication, and preparation for commercial binding. She has frequently served on national groups engaged in preservation studies and strategic plannning, collaborated in the development of conferences and workshops, served as a conference and classroom speaker, and published on a variety of preservation topics. Her current area of focus is the intersection of traditional and new preservation strategies and their appropriate application.

James G. Neal

At the time of the symposium, James G. Neal was dean of university libraries and Sheridan Director of the Milton S. Eisenhower Library at Johns Hopkins University. He is currently vice president for information services and university librarian at Columbia University. He served on the executive board of the American Library Association (ALA) and was president of the Association of Research Libraries in 1997–98. He represented the American library community as an adviser to the U.S. delegation at the World Intellectual Property Organization diplomatic conference on copyright in Geneva. Mr. Neal is a frequent speaker at national and international conferences and is a consultant and published researcher with a focus in the areas of organizational change, human resource development, scholarly communication, intellectual property, library fund-raising, and the impact of new technologies. He was selected 1997 Academic/Research Librarian of the Year by ALA's Association of College and Research Libraries.

Francis M. Ponti

Francis M. Ponti is research professor in statistics at the Columbian School of Arts and Sciences, the George Washington University, Washington, D.C., and statistical consultant to KPMG, LLP, on several federal government engagements, including the sampling plans for the Library of Congress. Dr. Ponti has wide government experience, most recently as technical director, Quantitative Methods Division, Department of Defense Inspector General (1986–97). He has also held a number of positions in operations research and training at the U.S. Office of Personnel Management and the U.S. Civil Service Commission. For his government work, he has received numerous awards, including the Secretary of Defense Medal for Meritorious Civilian Service, Department of Defense Inspector General

Citation for Distinguished Civilian Service, and the Director's Award, U.S. Office of Personnel Management. Dr. Ponti has considerable experience as a statistical consultant in private industry as well.

James M. Reilly

James M. Reilly is director of the Image Permanence Institute (IPI) at Rochester Institute of Technology in Rochester, New York. An academic research laboratory devoted to preservation technology and image preservation, IPI is cosponsored by the Society for Imaging Science and Technology. Mr. Reilly is the author of numerous technical articles on photograph and film preservation and has written two books, including *Care and Identification of 19th-Century Photographic Prints* (Rochester, N.Y. : Eastman Kodak Co., 1986). More recently, Mr. Reilly has worked in the areas of environmental assessment and institutional preservation and has been retained as a consultant by numerous museums, libraries, and archives.

Abby Smith

Abby Smith is director of programs at the Council on Library and Information Resources in Washington, D.C., which she joined in 1997. She is responsible for development and management of collaborative actions with key library and archival institutions to ensure long-term access to our cultural and scholarly heritage, including the creation of technical reports, newsletters, and other informational products that contribute to the analysis of preservation and access problems in all formats, including digital, and to their solution. From 1988 to 1997, she worked at the Library of Congress, first as a consultant to the special collections research divisions, then coordinating several cultural and academic programs in the office of the Librarian of Congress. As assistant to the Associate Librarian for Library Services, she directed a preservation microfilming program in the former Soviet Union, curated three exhibitions of Russian library and archival treasures from the former Soviet Union, and was curator and project director for the Library's first permanent exhibition of its holdings, *Treasures of the Library of Congress*. Dr. Smith has written and lectured widely on the subject of library preservation, the management of cultural assets, and the transformation of research institutions under the influence of new information technologies.

Laurie Sowd

As operations director at the Huntington Library, Art Collections, and Botanical Gardens, Laurie Sowd oversees security, facilities, information systems, risk management, safety, and emergency preparedness. She participates in an institution–wide task force aimed at improving visitor services at the museum. Ms. Sowd is on numerous boards and has spoken at national museum, library, and cultural property conferences on security, loss control, emergency preparedness, and technology topics.

James F. Williams, II

James F. Williams, II, has been dean of libraries at the University of Colorado at Boulder since 1988. His research interests include health sciences librarianship, strategic planning, collection development, leadership in research libraries, and resource sharing and networking. He has served on numerous boards, including the board of directors of the Association of Research Libraries. He is a member of the board of visitors for libraries at the Massachusetts Institute of Technology and the visiting committee at the School of Library and Information Science at the University of Pittsburgh. He has chaired the Association of College and Research Libraries K.G. Saur Award Committee and is currently a member of the editorial board of the journal *College and Research Libraries.*

INDEX

Index   275

preventive programs. *See also* preservation programs
   funding issues, 223
   importance of, xxi–xxii
   Library of Congress preservation framework, 87
printing negatives. *See* negatives; *specific formats*
print materials. *See also* acidic paper; *specific types of materials*
   collection building choices and, 136
   copyright issues, 205
   preservation funding history, 195
   preservation funding requirements, 153–54
   preservation history, 190
   preservation research, 142
   preservation techniques, 90–91, 101, 104, 247
   preservation technology decisions, 28–29
   research library preservation issues, 234–35
printout quality, digital reformatting issues, 180, 181, 186
privacy issues, 6
processing cycle
   Library of Congress preservation framework, 85, 87
   Library of Congress security program, 52, 53, 247
Professional Training Associates newsletter, 40–41
projection equipment, 213
Project RAPID, 133
property rights. *See* copyright issues
property thefts. *See* thefts
protection issues. *See specific headings beginning with* security
public libraries, 59, 142. *See also specific libraries and organizations*
public policy issues. *See* laws and legislation; U.S. Congress
public relations. *See also* news media
   benefits of openness, 13–14
   Colorado State University library flood, 131–32

Columbia University library thefts, 112–13, 119–20
FBI's Art Theft Program, 127
impact on programs, xxii
Library of Congress experiences, xx
raising interest in preservation and, 105
research library safety and security issues, 239
publishers. *See also* copyright issues
   digital reformatting issues, 104, 182, 191–92, 196–98, 203–5, 250
   national preservation efforts, 78

quality of programs. *See* effectiveness measurement; standards

radiation. *See* environmental conditions
radio-frequency-based library systems, 242
rare books. *See also* books; special collections; *specific collections and institutions*
   Columbia University library thefts, 13, 109–21, 247–48
   Library of Congress preservation framework, 84
   Library of Congress security program, 51, 53
   Library of Congress storage project, 174
   preservation funding strategies, 157
   preservation techniques, 96, 98
   preservation value issues, 227
   stewardship role and, 12, 15–16
readers. *See* patrons
reading equipment, 95, 167
rebinding. *See* binding and binderies
recording equipment, 213
recordings. *See* audiovisual materials
Reed-Scott, Jutta, 27–28
reference materials. *See also specific types of collections and materials*
   preservation techniques, 97
reference skills of staff, 6

staff pre-employment screening, 125, 239

staff recognition
    Denver Museum of Natural History, 40
    Science Place, 41
    suggestions for, 38

staff roles. *See also specific positions*
    clarifying, 14
    Colorado State University library, 130, 132, 137
    Columbia University, 112–13, 248
    conflicting library goals and, 5–7
    FBI's Art Theft Program, 125–26
    institutional priorities and, 9–11, 16
    interdepartmental contact and, 35, 37–38
    Library of Congress, xix–xx, 46–47, 86, 182
    preservation history, 179–80
    preservation techniques, 93–94
    preservation value issues, 227
    research library safety and security issues, 238–39
    security and preservation strategies, 15
    staff as clients, 37
    University of Maryland libraries, 59–60, 62–68

staff training
    Colorado State University library, 132, 137
    Huntington Library, Art Collections, and Botanical Gardens, 33–36
    Library of Congress, xx, 47–49
    preservation personnel, 74–75
    preservation techniques, 93–95, 98–100
    research library safety and security issues, 234, 239, 243
    research library stewardship issues, 232
    suggestions for, 39–40
    University of Maryland libraries, 59–60, 62–68

standards. *See also* effectiveness measurement
    collaboration suggestions, 252, 254
    for digital information, 80, 220, 242–43, 252
    for facilities, 252
    for microfilming, 101
    for security programs, 54–55, 67–68, 219

state laws. *See* laws and legislation

State University of New York at Buffalo, 75

statistical sampling, 163–67, 220, 249

status of materials, evaluating. *See* collection condition surveys; inventory control and tracking

statutes. *See* laws and legislation

stewardship. *See also specific aspects*
    copyright issues, 196
    description of, 3–4
    digital reformatting issues, 179
    preservation and security funding strategies, 155
    preservation issues and, 8–12, 14–17
    preservation techniques, 90
    research library issues and, 232–43, 250
    security issues and, 5–17
    stewardship reports, xix

storage areas and facilities. *See also* environmental conditions
    ARL survey findings, 144
    Colorado State University library, 134
    "fat factor" concept in water damage, 134
    Folger Shakespeare Library, 24–25
    Library of Congress, 47, 52, 88, 168, 173–74
    measuring environmental quality, 77–78, 168–75, 249
    national preservation efforts, 74, 256
    preservation and security strategies, 16
    preservation techniques, 91–93
    research libraries, 236, 238, 241

storage cycle

Library of Congress security program, xix, 49, 51–54, 56–57, 246
national preservation efforts, 236
preservation history, 179–80
preservation techniques, 101
research libraries, 222–31, 234–39, 250–51
research versus artifactual value, 224–25, 228–29, 231
surrogate copies and, 20–21, 28–29, 117–18, 182, 228
vandalism. *See* mutilation of collections; thefts
vaults. *See* storage areas and facilities
vendors, 134–35
ventilation. *See* environmental conditions
video cameras. *See also* closed-circuit television
research libraries, 242
security and preservation strategies, 15
University of Maryland libraries, 63, 65
videocassette recorders, 95
video materials. *See* audiovisual materials
video, streaming, 209, 211

vinegar syndrome, 24–25, 211, 246
visitors. *See also* accessibility issues; patrons; researchers
as clients, 37
conflicting library goals, 6–8
photography by, 6, 39

Washington, George, 114, 118
water damage
Colorado State University library, 130–38, 248
emergency response planning, 94
"fat factor" concept, 134
North Dakota State University library, 138
preservation technology decisions, 26
University of Maryland libraries, 66
valuation issues and, 11
Web sites. *See* Internet
wet materials. *See* water damage
Williams, Gordon, 72
Williams, James F. II, 250
Williams Report, 72
world's fair collection (Smithsonian), 146
World Wide Web. *See* Internet

Yates, Sidney, 76